The Archaeological Gu

Iowa and the Midwest Experience

SERIES EDITOR
William B. Friedricks,
Iowa History Center
at Simpson College

The
Archaeological
Guide
to Iowa

WILLIAM E. WHITTAKER

LYNN M. ALEX

MARY C. DE LA GARZA

University of Iowa Press, Iowa City

University of Iowa Press, Iowa City 52242

Copyright © 2015 by the University of Iowa Press

www.uiowapress.org

Printed in the United States of America

Design by April Leidig

The University of Iowa Press is a member of Green
Press Initiative and is committed to preserving
natural resources.

Printed on acid-free paper

ISBN: 978-1-60938-337-4 (pbk)
ISBN: 978-1-60938-338-1 (ebk)

Library of Congress Cataloging-in-Publication Data
is on file at the Library of Congress.

Cover art credits: *Clockwise, from top,* the Mississippi
River as seen from Effigy Mounds National Monument
(photo by Mary C. De La Garza/OSA); clam midden
excavation at the Palace site (photo by Mary C.
De La Garza/OSA); projectile points from the Kimball Village site (OSA); Blood Run site (photo by John
Pearson/Iowa Department of Natural Resources);
catlinite tablet found at the Blood Run site (image
adjustment by Carol Moxham/Midwest Archaeological
Center and Angela Collins/OSA; used courtesy of
Dale R. Henning and the OSA).

The land up north is too cold, and the land down south is too hot, and the land out west is too barren, nothing will grow, and the land out east is too bloody with our blood, nothing can grow. In Iowa I shall remain.

— MESKWAKI PROVERB

(Johnathan L. Buffalo,
 *A Short History of the
 Meskwaki*, 1989)

*Dedicated to Alan and LuAnne Becker,
devoted educators and preservationists.*

CONTENTS

ACKNOWLEDGMENTS

Many people and institutions helped produce this book.
Bob Burchfield, Catherine Cocks, John F. Doershuk,
Joseph A. Tiffany, Stephen C. Lensink, Shirley J. Schermer,
David M. Gradwohl, Nancy Osborn Johnsen, Cynthia
Peterson, Bill L. Quackenbush, Gail Barels, John Pearson,
Matthew Donovan, Donald Gaff, Alan Nelson, and an
unknown reviewer provided resources and useful comments;
their help is deeply appreciated. Financial support came
from the Iowa Archeological Society and the University of
Iowa's Office for the Vice President of Research. The Office
of the State Archaeologist (OSA) provided substantial
research support for the project. All images used in this
book are from the OSA collections, unless noted otherwise.
Artifacts are not shown to scale. Copies of all references in
this book may be found on file at the OSA.

Introduction

IN 1963, ARCHAEOLOGISTS exploring the remains of Fort Madison found something curious. Among the debris in the foundation of the officers' quarters, they discovered a stone spear point. This point was typical of the Early to Middle Woodland periods, roughly 2,000 years ago, and an officer presumably collected it from somewhere nearby. Left behind in 1813 as Fort Madison (68*) was hastily abandoned during an Indian siege, this point represents the first known artifact collected in Iowa. It would not be the last. Public interest in Iowa's archaeological past had begun.

Today there are approximately 27,000 recorded archaeological sites in Iowa, although most people are unaware of and would pay little attention to the vast majority. Ranging in significance from the 100 mounds at Sny Magill in Effigy Mounds National Monument (47) to small scatters of recent historic trash noted during highway surveys, most sites consist of old abandoned farmsteads or small scatters of prehistoric flakes and heated rocks, with little information known about them beyond their location and their meager contents. Many sites, in fact, are completely gone or badly disturbed—destroyed by plowing, by erosion, or by roads and other development.

Fortunately, there are sites that the public can visit directly or can learn about from nearby interpretive exhibits. Fewer things are more inspiring than walking among the Malchow Mounds (66), packed so tightly it is hard to tell where one mound ends and the other begins. Strolling around downtown Des Moines (23) is different when you are aware of the mounds, the Indian villages, and the fort that once stood there. And while you cannot visit the Wanampito site (31), you can see the splendid 17th-century protohistoric artifacts at Heery Woods State Park.

For those who want to experience archaeological places firsthand, the 68 sites described here provide an opportunity. Many can be visited, can be seen from a public location, or have artifact collections on display. A

*Numbers reflect order of sites as listed in this book, see map and key on pages 8–9.

1

few are important sites included because of the unique story they tell, but their exact location is not revealed, some because they are gone, like the Old Pacific City Cemetery (14), some because they are on secluded private property, like the Poisel site (67). We intentionally chose to include sites in every corner of the state and to diversify the types of sites. We avoided the temptation of including every mound site. Although often the most aesthetically interesting sites, mounds tell only part of the story of Iowa's past.

The order in which sites are presented follows Iowa's river systems, generally from west to east, and then from north to south. Large rivers appear to have been the highways of prehistoric people, and similar site types often cluster along specific river systems. For example, the Late Prehistoric Mill Creek village sites (3, 4, 6, 7, 8) tend to congregate along the Little Sioux and Big Sioux Rivers in northwest Iowa.

Sites are identified by name and occasionally by a recorded site number. Often the person who recorded an archaeological site named it, typically using the landowner's name, a nearby geographic feature, or an association with a historic event. Thus the Kimball site (3) retains an earlier landowner's name, while Blood Run (2) references the creek that cuts across the site. Recently, the Office of the State Archaeologist (OSA) has solicited input from the Native American community in naming sites that might be tied to specific tribes, such as Wanampito (31).

All recorded sites in Iowa are given a site number by the OSA, following a system called the Smithsonian Trinomial, devised in the 1930s. In Iowa, site numbers begin with "13," since Iowa was the 13th state alphabetically before Alaska and Hawaii became states. After "13," there is a two-letter county abbreviation, followed by the number of the site as it was recorded in that county; 13BH3 (33), for instance, represents the third site recorded in Blackhawk County, Iowa.

Each site has an intriguing history, and in telling it we draw directly from the reports and publications of the original researchers. Charles R. Keyes and his assistant, Ellison Orr, sometimes anointed the "founding fathers" of Iowa archaeology, stand out as the two most important early researchers. Their personal endeavors and decades of work, particularly for the Iowa Archaeological Survey beginning in 1922, established the basic groundwork for understanding Iowa's prehistoric past and furthered the protection and preservation of many sites (see Weed Park Mounds [62]).

Dozens of archaeologists at public institutions and private organizations throughout Iowa and beyond contribute annually to our collective knowledge of the state's history, including the OSA, our own home base. Equally valuable to our understanding of Iowa's past is the historical perspective of descendant communities. While we have not presumed to speak for these descendants, their ancestors were responsible for much of the archaeological record described here.

This book uses the terms "Indian," "Native American," "Native," and "American Indian" interchangeably, as do Native communities themselves. In general, tribal names are spelled the way modern tribes spell them, if there is a chance of confusion; other names by which some groups were known are also given, for example, the Ho-Chunk (Winnebago).

The term "prehistoric" is used throughout the book. Its original meaning, "before written text," has been lost to the modern meaning of history as "everything recorded in the past." Many Indians do not like "prehistoric" or "protohistoric" because these terms imply that Indians do not have oral records of the past, which they certainly do, and their use defines Indians by their relationship to Europeans. However, alternative terms, such as "precontact" and "pre-Columbian," also define Indians by their relationship to Europeans; there is no perfect term to use at this time.

Cultural Periods in Iowa Archaeology

PALEOINDIAN PERIOD (13,500–10,500 years ago)

If you were to walk across Iowa with the first humans known to have lived here, the scene would resemble the Yukon more than Des Moines. The glaciers were receding 13,000 years ago, and Iowa was covered by tundra and forests. A large glacier, the Des Moines Lobe, still covered much of north-central Iowa.

The oldest artifacts found in Iowa are Clovis points, which have been found throughout the state. Although popular belief holds that Paleoindians were big-game hunters stalking mammoths and mastodons, research suggests that most of their food likely came from small game and wild plants. So far, there are no definitive early Paleoindian sites in Iowa with preserved features such as hearths or houses. Paleoindians were fairly mobile, and probably did not create large sites. The sites they made in Iowa have either decayed or eroded away, leaving only stone artifacts, or are very deeply buried in river valleys. Numerous sites have Paleoindian spear points or other evidence of late Paleoindian occupation, such as the Five Island Lake site (16).

ARCHAIC PERIOD (10,500–2,800 years ago)

Most of Iowa's prehistory is included in the Archaic period. During the Archaic, humans shifted toward hunting and gathering within smaller territories and built increasingly larger sites, which they occupied seasonally. The climate during the Archaic changed over time. A gradual warming of the climate in the Early Archaic led toward the establishment of ecosystems not unlike modern conditions. At the Hypsithermal peak, a worldwide period of warming that climaxed about 6,000–8,000 years ago, Iowa was warmer and dryer, more like Kansas is today, but then the climate gradually cooled back to modern conditions. Toward the end of the Archaic, pottery making, plant cultivation, and mound building began. In western Iowa, bison hunting appears to be a major source of food and materials, as seen at the Cherokee Sewer site (9). In central and eastern Iowa, sites were larger and more complex, as seen at the Palace (24), McNeal Fan (63), and Edgewater Park (39) sites. The earliest known human burials occur at Middle Archaic sites like Palace and Turin (11). The best evidence for early house structures comes from Middle Archaic sites such as Palace, with a Middle Archaic village identified at McNeal Fan.

WOODLAND PERIOD (800 B.C.–A.D. 1250)

The Woodland period is known for domestic plants, pottery, and mounds, all things that actually appeared at the end of the Late Archaic, and for increasing numbers of more settled communities occupying defined territories. The shift away from hunting and gathering to agriculture was slow, and wild foods would always remain important to prehistoric Iowans.

Woodland mounds are probably the most spectacular sites to visit. Large Woodland mound groups are found at Effigy Mounds National Monument (47) and the Malchow Mounds (66). In northeast Iowa, enigmatic animal-shaped mounds can be found at Effigy Mounds National Monument and Pikes Peak (48), and an odd cruciform-shaped (cross-shaped) mound is at Folkert (30). Mounds were also recorded early in unexpected places, such as downtown Des Moines (23) and Fort Dodge (17).

Rockshelters and caves often have good preservation, and excavations at sites like Ginger Stairs (37), Maquoketa (58), the Jackson County rockshelters (59), and Woodpecker Cave (38) revealed important information about the Woodland diet and lifeways.

The Early and Middle Woodland periods appear to have been times of social flourishing. Near the Mississippi valley, Early Woodland Indians built large burial mounds and traded exotic raw material over long distances. The burials at Turkey River (54) indicate a complex social realm. Archaeologists excavated several Early Woodland houses at McNeal Fan (63), revealing glimpses of daily life. During the Middle Woodland period, Indians in eastern Iowa participated in the Havana and Hopewell interaction networks, obtaining copper from the Great Lakes, shell from the Gulf Coast, and obsidian from the Rockies. The elaborate rattlesnake shell gorget excavated at Hadfields Cave (58) may represent one of these trade items. Early and Middle Woodland enclosures may have been present at Poisel (67), Turkey River (54), and Toolesboro (65).

The Late Woodland period does not display the same degree of long-distance interaction and trade as the Early and Middle Woodland periods, but Late Woodland sites are common, such as the Dee Norton site (41). True arrowheads, thinner ceramics, and new crops, including maize, appeared, but agriculture was small scale, and people appear to have depended on highly localized hunting and gathering. Late Woodland sites suggest a steady increase in population and regional variation. It is likely that many of the small sites with conical mounds in Iowa date to the Late Woodland period, such as Fish Farm Mounds (44), Four Mounds (55), Harpers Cemetery (45), Weed Park (62), Vegors Cemetery (18), Wickiup Hill (34), and Woodland Mounds Preserve (25). It was during this time that the effigy mounds characterize northeast Iowa.

LATE PREHISTORIC PERIOD (A.D. 900–1600)

Maize farming appeared in the Woodland period in Iowa, but it intensified in the Late Prehistoric period, perhaps because more productive and robust corn varieties emerged. A ridged Late Prehistoric field still exists at the Litka site (7). Maize farming may have allowed the human population to increase, and this increase in population likely led to large villages. In Iowa, there is a split between east and west in the Late Prehistoric period. Western Iowa sites in the Missouri River basin made the transition to village life earlier, and had closer cultural ties to people on the Plains. In western Iowa, rectangular earth and timber lodges appeared about 1,000 years ago. Substantial semisubterranean houses excavated at Davis-Oriole (12) and other sites near Glenwood (13) are considered part of the Central Plains tradition and may be associated with historically known Plains tribes such as the Arikara and Pawnee. Compact village sites in northwest Iowa fortified with ditches and an earthen berm, such as Kimball Village (3), Double Ditch (6), and Wittrock (8), are placed within the Middle Missouri tradition. The people living at Mill Creek sites may be, in part, the ancestors of later Plains tribes such as the Hidatsa and Mandan.

In eastern Iowa, the Late Woodland lasted longer and was eventually replaced by people of the Oneota tradition. Large enclosed villages appear, such as those along the Upper Iowa River (43) and perhaps at 13BH3 (33) and Rice Lake (29). Oneota people were living in western Iowa at sites like Dixon (10) by the 1300s. The people associated with Oneota sites in Iowa are the likely ancestors of historically known tribes, such as the Ioway, Otoe, Missouria, Ho-Chunk (Winnebago), Kansa, Osage, and possibly the Omaha-Ponca. At least three Oneota sites once stood in what is now downtown Des Moines (23).

PROTOHISTORIC PERIOD (A.D. 1600–1800)

The Oneota cultures were the first observed by European explorers and traders. Indians began to acquire European goods, and large population shifts occurred because of disease and migration during the protohistoric period, so called because it typically lacks the written accounts of the later historic period. Warfare pushed eastern Algonquian language–speaking tribes such as the Illinois, Sauk, Meskwaki, and Potawatomi into Iowa.

Protohistoric sites often emerged from Oneota sites, such as Blood Run (2) and Wanampito (31). As contact with Europeans increased in the protohistoric, archaeological sites were dominated by European trade goods, and Native ceramic forms and stone projectile points became uncommon, such as the Mines of Spain complex (56).

HISTORIC PERIOD (post-A.D. 1800)

After Marquette and Joliet paddled down the Mississippi in 1673, written accounts of the land that would be Iowa increasingly help to flesh out the archaeological record. Because such accounts existed for some parts of the state earlier than for others, the historic period also begins at different times in different places.

Sergeant Charles Floyd (5), one member of the Lewis and Clark expedition, was buried in Iowa, and references to Iowaville (27) occur in the Corps of Discovery's maps and journals and on other early maps. As the newly formed United States tried to assert control over the region, the government built forts to dissuade occupation by foreign forces, especially the British. Fort Madison (68), the scene of the only true military battle in Iowa, has well-preserved early historic deposits, including a battlefield buried under a parking lot. Other forts explored archaeologically include Fort Atkinson (50), Fort Dodge (17), and Fort Des Moines (23). As resident and new Indian peoples were pushed through Iowa prior to Euroamerican settlement, trading posts such as Hewitt-Olmstead (51) and Patterson (35) were built to accommodate (and exploit) them. The earliest settlers included some famous figures, including Governor Robert Lucas, who lived at Plum Grove (40), and the early trader/pioneer/entrepreneur Antoine LeClaire (61). The Amana fish weir (36) was probably constructed during this time. Early towns and industry included the Bonaparte Pottery (28), the African American community at Buxton (26), the Elgin Brewery (52), Hurstville (60), and the Motor townsite (53). Sites where historic events occurred include the Hitchcock House (15), a stop on the Underground Railroad; Jesse Hoover's blacksmith shop (42), where young Herbert Hoover played; and Terrace Hill, today's governor's residence (22). Other interesting sites include the veterinary carcass pit at Iowa State University (20) and the Bowen's Prairie townsite and associated cheese factory (57).

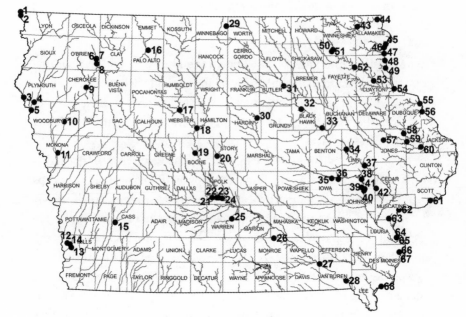

Numbers denote site locations as listed in the book. The numbering system follows Iowa's river systems, generally from west to east and then north to south.

1 Gitchie Manitou

2 Blood Run National Historic Landmark

3 Kimball Village

4 Cowan Site

5 Sergeant Floyd's Grave

6 Double Ditch

7 Litka Ridged Field Site

8 Wittrock Indian Village

9 Cherokee Sewer Site

10 Dixon Site

11 Turin

12 Davis-Oriole Site

13 Glenwood Archaeological State Preserve

14 Pacific City Cemetery

15 Hitchcock House

16 Five Island Lake

17 Fort Dodge Military Post

18 Vegors Cemetery

19 Boone Mound

20 Iowa State Veterinary Carcass Pit

21 West Des Moines Burial Site

22 Terrace Hill

23 Des Moines Urban Archaeology

24 Palace Site

25 Woodland Mounds State Preserve

26 Buxton

27 Iowaville

28 Bonaparte Pottery

29 Des Moines Lobe Sites

30 Folkert Mound Group

31 Wanampito Site

32 Black Medicine Site

33 Cedar Valley Nature Trail

34 Wickiup Hill

35 Patterson Trading Post

36 Amana Fish Weir

37 Ginger Stairs

38 Woodpecker Cave

39 Edgewater Park Site

40 Plum Grove

41 Hickory Hill Park

42 Herbert Hoover National Historic Site

43 Upper Iowa Enclosures

44 Fish Farm Mounds

45 Harpers Ferry Mound Group

46 Paint Rock

47 Effigy Mounds

48 Pike's Peak

49 Sny Magill

50 Fort Atkinson

51 Hewitt-Olmstead Trading Post

52 Elgin Brewery

53 Motor Town

54 Turkey River Mound Group

55 Four Mounds

56 Mines of Spain

57 Oneida Cheese Factory

58 Hadfields Cave

59 Jackson County Rockshelters

60 Hurstville Lime Kilns

61 Antoine LeClaire House

62 Weed Park Mounds

63 McNeal Fan Site

64 McKinney Site

65 Toolesboro Mounds National Historic Landmark

66 Malchow Mounds

67 Poisel Mounds

68 Fort Madison

Visiting Sites

Site locations are typically protected for a number of reasons: to safeguard them from vandals, to prevent trespassing on private property, and to preserve sites considered sacred to Native Americans. On the other hand, revealing site locations can help to protect sites, since it discourages in-advertent damage caused by ignorance and increases appreciation for ar-chaeological resources as a whole, which is important for their preservation.

In this book, we did our best to direct the reader to sites that are generally well known and already publicly accessible. In some cases, the site has been so thoroughly excavated or otherwise destroyed that only its former loca-tion can be visited. With the exception of mound sites, most prehistoric sites listed here have no visible traces left on the surface. They lie in woods and fields, under city streets and industrial areas. Often they are deep below ground, sometimes detectable as a stone flake or a piece of fire-cracked rock eroded along a trail. Historic sites are often more visible; they may display cellar depressions, building foundations, old trails, lilac bushes surviving in locations where they were planted, and scatters of crockery and brick fragments.

Some Iowa sites have been designated as National Historic Landmarks (NHLs), many are listed on the National Register of Historic Places (NRHP), and a number are incorporated into the Iowa State Preserve System. The Na-tional Park Service oversees both the NHL and the NRHP programs, both federally designated programs that recognize and acknowledge significant historic properties, thus highlighting the importance of their preservation. The Iowa State Preserve System began in 1965 to preserve Iowa's natural, prehistoric, and historic heritage. A site qualifying for preserve status re-ceives the highest level of protection offered by the state.

Even now most states, including Iowa, lack legislation that safeguards archaeological sites. Aside from laws protecting graves, and by extension prehistoric mounds, no Iowa statute requires the protection of significant historic or prehistoric sites on private property. Even an NHL or a site listed on the NHRP is not protected. Such designations offer a level of recognition for the historical significance of a site that might be taken into consider-ation in the face of certain types of threats.

If you see artifacts, historic or prehistoric, leave them where you found them. Their temporary value to you as a souvenir is lessened with the knowledge that you are destroying a bit of the past. Only when found in context (in situ) can that artifact ever begin to fully tell what happened at the site.

Respect private property; if the site is on private land, stay on public roads. While mounds are interesting to look at, please don't walk on them; this flattens the surface and damages the vegetation that protects the mound.

In Iowa, it is illegal to knowingly dig into any suspected human burial site, including mounds, and it is illegal to dig into archaeological sites on public lands. If you think you see human remains exposed at a site, call the OSA immediately (319-384-0732); if you see someone digging illegally at an archaeological site, call the police and then call the OSA.

If you know of the location of archaeological sites, do not hesitate to contact the OSA (osa@uiowa.edu). Every year the public helps document dozens of new sites, some of them spectacular. In 2013, the OSA recorded a group of nine mounds in Des Moines County and a bear effigy mound in Allamakee County. The locations of most archaeological sites are generally kept confidential by the OSA, and sites on private property are not disclosed to the public without the owner's permission. If you own a mound or other archaeological site, contact the OSA if you want more information about the site and advice on how to preserve it.

To learn more about Iowa archaeology, Lynn M. Alex's *Iowa's Archaeological Past* (University of Iowa Press, 2000) remains the standard reference. Lance Foster's *The Indians of Iowa* (University of Iowa Press, 2009) is a good introduction to the Indian tribes that lived in the state. There are a number of websites of interest as well. Some direct you to other public locations where archaeological sites exist.

* Iowa Archeological Society: www.uiowa.edu/~osa/IAS
* Facebook: www.facebook.com/IowaArchaeology
* Office of the State Archaeologist: archaeology.uiowa.edu
* State Historical Society of Iowa: www.iowahistory.org
* Iowa Museums: www.iowamuseums.org
* Iowa Archaeology on *Wikipedia*: en.wikipedia.org/wiki/Iowa_archaeology
  (most of the content was developed by the authors of this book)

* Crops of Ancient Iowa:
  http://archaeology.uiowa.edu/crops-ancient-iowa
* Association of Iowa Archaeologists:
  archaeology.uiowa.edu/association-iowa-archaeologists
  (lists professional archaeologists in Iowa)
* National Historic Landmarks Program: http://www.nps.gov/nhl/
* Iowa State Preserves: www.iowadnr.gov/Destinations/StatePreserves
* Effigy Mounds National Monument: www.nps.gov/efmo
* Loess Hills Archaeological Interpretive Center:
  loesshillsarchaeology.org
* Sanford Museum: www.sanfordmuseum.org
* Department of Anthropology, University of Iowa:
  clas.uiowa.edu/anthropology
* Department of Anthropology, Iowa State University:
  www.anthr.iastate.edu
* Department of Anthropology, Grinnell College:
  www.grinnell.edu/academic/anthropology
* Department of Anthropology, Luther College: anthropology.luther.edu

1 Gitchie Manitou—
Indian Mounds or Rebuilt Mounds?

✳ *Lyon County*

✳ *Woodland or Late Prehistoric*

✳ SITE NUMBER 13LO401

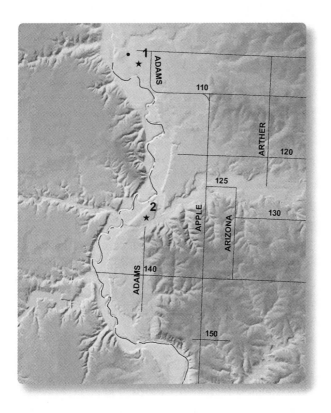

FAR NORTHWEST IOWA is best known for the Blood Run site, a complex of mounds, earthworks, and protohistoric and prehistoric structures that covers a swath of Lyon County and extends into South Dakota (see Blood Run [2]). To the north of Blood Run is a smaller group of 17 mounds, the northwesternmost in Iowa and just a few hundred yards from where the state's northern border intersects the Big Sioux River. Known in Ojibwa as "Gitchie Manitou," interpreted as "great spirit," the mounds were surveyed by Theodore H. Lewis in 1889.

13

Mound at Gitchie Manitou State Preserve, Lyon County. Photo by Joe Artz, EarthView Environmental, Inc. Courtesy of the Iowa Department of Natural Resources.

This small corner of northwest Lyon County is the only Iowa bedrock source of Sioux quartzite, an extremely hard and pretty pink rock historically used for building and paving stones. The oldest bedrock in Iowa, 1.6 billon years old, it was laid down during the period when single-cell life forms began to evolve into multicellular life. Originally the state bought the site for a quarry, but in the 1930s the Works Progress Administration (WPA) turned it into a park with a beautiful shelter house made of Sioux quartzite. In 1969, Gitchie Manitou was dedicated as a state preserve.

While other archaeological sites occur within the boundaries of Gitchie Manitou, the mounds have never been excavated, and no points or pottery have been collected from them, so we do not know if they are related to Blood Run or if they are older Woodland mounds. In fact, until recently, it was not clear if these mounds were the original prehistoric mounds or if they were rebuilt. When Roye Lindsay, of the University of Nebraska, visited the site in 1970, he noted the mounds were very low and almost imperceptible, except when they were highlighted by blowing snow, but they were in seemingly good condition. However, when he spoke with local informants, he found that they questioned the mounds' authenticity, noting that "there is some local controversy as to the antiquity of these mounds. Local residents indicate they were built by the W.P.A. during the 1930s. Another informant, of Doon, Iowa, indicated that the workmen had merely shoveled dirt on existing high spots assumed to be mounds."

While Lewis clearly saw mounds here in 1889, it is possible that farmers plowed them away to the extent that they were barely perceptible in the 1930s. The oldest aerial photograph of the site, dating from the 1930s, shows the north part of the mound group under plow, the rest pasture. Did the WPA really rebuild the mounds or add to them? If it did add to the mounds, why are they still so low?

These mounds, like all mounds, may contain human burials, so they are protected and cannot be excavated (see Old Pacific City Cemetery [14]). However, if there is a question as to whether a mound is prehistoric, the OSA Burials Program can test it using a small-diameter soil core, less than an inch wide. A soils specialist, called a geomorphologist, compares the different soil levels of the mound for color, texture, structure, and rock inclusions, and can infer the age of the mounds by comparing the mound soil to soil from off the mound. A mound built in the 1930s should have clearly disturbed soils, but a mound built 1,000 years ago should have better-developed soils.

After numerous soil cores taken on and off the mounds, the results of a 2013 geomorphological study at Gitchie Manitou by Joe Artz confirmed that prehistoric people had created the mounds in the state preserve, and there was no evidence that they were rebuilt in the 1930s.

✴ TO VISIT

Gitchie Manitou State Preserve is located near the Big Sioux River in far northwest Lyon County, southeast of Sioux Falls, South Dakota. From Sioux Falls, take State Highway 42 east. Turn south on 481st Avenue, east on the state line road (called variously County Highway 150, 268th Street, or 100th Street), and south on Adams Avenue, also called County Highway K10. The nearest Iowa town is Larchwood; take State Highway 9 west, turn west on the state line road (called variously County Highway 150, 268th Street, or 100th Street), then south on Adams Avenue, also called County Highway K10.

There is parking just off Adams Avenue. Remember that all mounds are protected by state law. If you keep following the trail, you will find the imposing ruins of the old WPA shelter house.

✳ WANT TO LEARN MORE?

Artz, Joe Alan

2014   Geoarchaeological Probing of Mounds at 13L0402, Gitchie Manitou State Preserve, Lyon County, Iowa. Prepared for the Iowa Department of Natural Resources, Des Moines, Iowa. EarthView Environmental, Inc., Coralville, Iowa.

Herzberg, Ruth, and John Pearson

2001   *The Guide to Iowa's State Preserves.* Iowa City: University of Iowa Press.

Lindsay, Roye D.

1970   *An Appraisal of Archaeological Resources in the Canton Reservoir, Northwest Iowa.* Lincoln: Department of Anthropology, University of Nebraska, Lincoln.

2 Blood Run/Rock Island: A National Historic Landmark without Equal

✳ *Lyon County, Iowa, and Lincoln County, South Dakota*

✳ *Late Prehistoric and Protohistoric*

✳ SITE NUMBER 13LO2

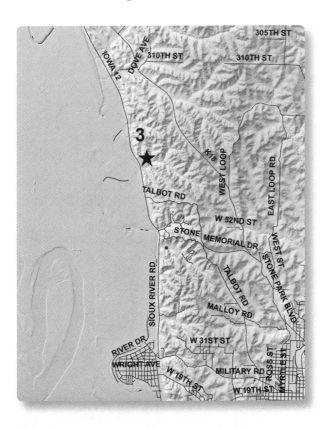

NAMED FOR A CREEK that runs through the property, Blood Run National Historic Landmark encompasses more than 1.3 square miles along both sides of the Big Sioux River straddling the Iowa–South Dakota border. The South Dakota portion is called the Rock Island site. Numerous peoples lived, visited, or passed through here as early as the Middle Archaic, 6,500 years ago, and probably earlier. The magnitude of human activity between

Pitted boulder, Blood Run National Historic Landmark, Lyon County.

Shaded relief map created from lidar image showing mound locations, Blood Run National Historic Landmark, Lyon County.

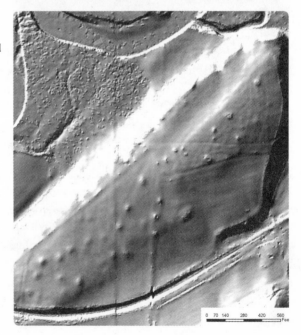

A.D. 1500 and 1700, however, eclipses all that came before. And yet this site remains virtually unknown.

Tribal accounts, early documents, and French maps identify Omaha/ Ponca peoples living at Blood Run by the late 1600s. These sources, backed by archaeological evidence, also link the site with the Ioway and Otoe, and possibly the Arikara, Cheyenne, and Dakota, who occasionally visited the site. Distinctive artifacts associated with these peoples, particularly pottery, as well as European trade items confirm this as a place touched by many. When European traders and explorers visited the region in the early 1700s, they found the site all but abandoned. Archaeologists generally agree that pressure from Dakota tribes forced previous residents to flee Blood Run before 1714. By 1851, Dakota peoples also relinquished this portion of Iowa to American settlers.

Referred to as *Xe* (pronounced "*khay*"), "where something is buried," by Ioway and Otoe peoples, Blood Run is actually a complex of site features that includes earthen burial mounds, stone circles possibly outlining former lodges, and large pitted boulders—enormous rocks with hundreds of fist-sized indentations covering their surface. Nineteenth-century accounts also describe the existence of an oval-shaped earthen embankment covering 15 acres and a serpent-shaped mound, neither confirmed by later researchers, but both vanished today.

Limited archaeological excavations in the 1960s and 1980s identified Blood Run as a Late Prehistoric/protohistoric Oneota site (see the McKinney site [64]). The discoveries, including burials, confirmed the presence of abundant Native-made and European-made artifacts. People living here received European trade items before Europeans visited the site. The tremendous amount of pipestone (catlinite) artifacts, in all stages of manufacture, suggests Native artisans at Blood Run made pipes, pendants, and plaques to trade throughout the Midwest. Access to the catlinite quarries at today's Pipestone National Monument in Minnesota, less than 50 miles away, helps explain the site's location and its complexity.

Blood Run is the largest and most complex protohistoric Oneota site known, forming a cultural landscape without parallel. Although plowing, a railroad track, a quarry, and antiquarian collecting and digging destroyed many of the site's original features, a hike across this timeless landscape still evokes a haunting sense of its past. Dozens of mounds, now protected by Iowa law (see Old Pacific City Cemetery [14]), a handful of pitted boulders, and numerous stone circles hidden in the sod and prairie grass remain. In 1970, the site was designated a National Historic Landmark, and in 1987 the State Historical Society of Iowa, in cooperation with the Iowa Natural Heritage Foundation, acquired approximately 230 acres of the site's core area.

Today, descendant peoples and local communities have joined state and national organizations to devise ways to further understand and protect Blood Run. It offers unparalleled opportunities to reveal exceptional insight into Native technology, settlement, ceremonial practices, and trade at a time of drastic and unalterable change in the lives of its residents.

✳ TO VISIT

Blood Run is southeast of Sioux Falls, South Dakota. The Iowa portion is administered by the State Historical Society of Iowa. From Iowa County Road A26 near Larchwood, take County Road K12, then turn west. Turn north on County Road A18, then west on K10. To visit the Iowa portion of the site, a guided tour by the Lyon County Conservation Board is recommended (712-472-2217), or visit www.iowahistory.org/shsi/historic-sites /blood-run.

Parts of the site in South Dakota have been incorporated into Good Earth State Park southeast of Sioux Falls. The nearby Gitchie Manitou site (1) could be considered part of the Blood Run complex.

✳ WANT TO LEARN MORE?

Henning, Dale R., and Gerald F. Schnepf
2012 *Blood Run: The Silent City.* Booklet sponsored by the Lyon County Historical Society and the U.S. National Park Service.

Henning, Dale R., and Thomas D. Thiessen, eds.
2004 *Dhegihan and Chiwere Siouans in the Plains: Historical and Archaeological Perspectives.* Memoir 36. *Plains Anthropologist* 49, no. 192, Part 2.

Peterson, Cynthia L., Melanie A. Riley, Kurtis H. Kettler,
and Melody K. Pope
2012   *Blood Run National Historic Landmark Documentation Improvement and
Preliminary Boundary Study*. Contract Completion Report 1959.
Office of the State Archaeologist, University of Iowa, Iowa City.

Wedel, Mildred Mott
1974   Le Sueur and the Dakota Sioux. In *Aspects of Upper Great Lakes
Anthropology*, ed. Elden Johnson, 157–171. St. Paul: Minnesota
Historical Society.
1981   The Ioway, Oto, and Omaha Indians in 1700. *Journal of the Iowa
Archeological Society* 28:1–13.

3 Kimball Village

 ✳ *Plymouth County*

 ✳ *Late Prehistoric*

 ✳ SITE NUMBER 13PM4

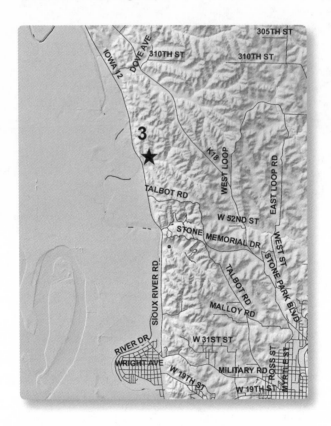

WAS NORTHWEST IOWA a dangerous place 800 years ago? The introduction of highly productive varieties of corn to the Missouri River basin may have allowed the growth of the human population and the appearance of fortified and permanent villages. After millennia of living in small, short-term sites, indigenous people began to live in large sites with substantial houses. The Kimball Village, north of Sioux City in the floodplain of the Big Sioux River, was so densely occupied that it may be a rare North American example of a tell, an archaeological site that has been occupied so intensively and long enough that the repeated occupations created a small hill. Archaeologists call the people who left the tell behind the Mill Creek culture (see Double Ditch [6], Wittrock [8], and Litka [7]).

Rather than live in widely separated earthlodges, like their Glenwood neighbors to the south, people of the Mill Creek culture instead chose to live in tightly packed settlements, with earthlodges abutting one another, surrounded by a ditch and wall. Village sites include Kimball, Wittrock, Chan-ya-ta, Bultman, Lange, and Double Ditch, all near the Big Sioux and Little Sioux Rivers. Possible descendants of the Mill Creek site occupants include the Hidatsa and Mandan, who built fortified villages in the Missouri River basin well into the historic period.

In 1939, Ellison Orr excavated two large trenches and several smaller units at the Kimball Village site. The largest trench was 152 feet long. He expanded this trench after he found rows of holes where posts once stood associated with houses at the base of the mound, about 8 feet below surface. He also excavated part of three houses at Kimball Village, spaced 12 feet apart in a row with central hearths and storage pits. Because his other large trench did not encounter house features, he speculated that a plaza stood at the center of the village. He noticed that in contrast to the houses of the Glenwood culture (see Glenwood Archaeological State Preserve [13] and Davis-Oriole [12]), which were semisubterranean, with their floors excavated into the ground, along the Big Sioux River house floors were level with the surrounding ground. Orr did not screen for artifacts or make detailed notes of soils, and appears to have paid little attention to the fill between the top and the bottom of the mound. As a result, it is not clear if the 8 feet of soil above the house remnants he found was washed in by the river or represented a legacy of later human activity. He did diagram the general profile of the mound and revealed that it was probably built on top of a natural rise.

The artifacts Orr recovered were spectacular. He found complete pots, several of which had handles shaped like animal effigies. Worked bone artifacts, including awls, squash knives, fishhooks, chisels, scoops, pins, beads, and needles, were common. The hundreds of stone artifacts he uncovered included hide scrapers, drills, knives, and arrow points. Many of the artifacts were works of art, among them carved catlinite pipes and bone, shell and stone beads, and mussel shells carved into fish shapes.

Kimball site excavation, 1939, Plymouth County. Courtesy of the State Historical Society of Iowa, Iowa City, Charles R. Keyes Archaeological Collection, and the University of Iowa Office of the State Archaeologist.

In 1963, archaeologists, including Dale R. Henning and Walter Klippel, returned to the site. Henning excavated a few small units at the southern tip of the mound. While he also did not study soils in detail, he noted stratified soils, and he found features and artifacts above the base of the mound, suggesting the mound had been constructed by humans, not by floodwaters. Klippel found a bison bone concentration, three storage pits, and a human burial.

In 2009, with better understanding of soils and stratigraphy, the University of Arkansas and the OSA reinvestigated the mound, attempting to do so in a less invasive way. Instead of excavation blocks, the OSA excavated a line of deep augers, made detailed profiles from several soil cores, and produced a detailed topographic map. Kenneth Kvamme, of the University of Arkansas, surveyed the mound with a barrage of instruments, from ground-penetrating radar to resistivity, conductivity, and magnetic gradiometry (see Double Ditch [6]).

The soil cores revealed a deeply stratified site with very subtle changes in the soil that suggest the mound was built up during at least four occupations. Each occupation draped the previous occupation and likely disturbed older occupations. Since the soils were subtly different in the mound fill, they would not have been obvious to Orr, whereas the features at the base of the mound cut into the natural soils and were easy to discern. Soil coring and augering also found evidence of a ditch around the mound, as well as deep pits and hearths. Unlike earlier excavations, the 2009 effort involved screening soils from all levels and found artifacts throughout the fill. Several ceramic styles were noted although no apparent change occurred in the ratio of styles between upper and lower parts of the mound, indicating cultural continuity during the different occupations. Kvamme's magnetic gradiometry survey revealed as many as 21 possible houses in the mound and confirmed that a ditch probably surrounded the mound. Comparisons between Orr's cross-mound profile and modern profiles reveal the mound is slowly being eroded by plowing, the edges of the tell are being eaten away, and the mound is less well defined.

There are many unanswered questions about Kimball Mound. Are the houses Kvamme saw close to the surface or deeper? All the radiocarbon dates came from items uncovered at the base of the mound; how different would dates be from upper parts of the mound? Could a sequence of houses be detected if the site were more carefully excavated? How does the mound change over time? If there were several occupations, why did the occupants keep building up the mound? Was flooding a problem? Was there serious threat of attack from enemies, or was living in houses close to each other on a rise surrounded by a ditch a sign of the residents' unity? If this was a tight-knit society, why were there storage pits inside houses, instead of communal storage pits? While many of these questions will probably never be answered, the tell itself has been nominated as a National Historic Landmark, a designation that would recognize its importance and help to preserve it for the future.

✳ TO VISIT

The Kimball Mound is privately owned, and visitors are not allowed. Drive north on Highway 12 along the Big Sioux River to the new archaeological state preserve, on the east side of the highway just north of Sioux City, to experience the landscape in the region of the Kimball site. At the Dorothy Pecaut Nature Center, 4500 Sioux River Road, Sioux City (712-258-0838), and the Sioux City Public Museum, 607 4th Street, Sioux City (712-279-6174), you can see artifacts from the Kimball site and interpretive exhibits about Mill Creek culture.

✳ WANT TO LEARN MORE?

Henning, Dale R., Amy E. Henning, and David A. Baerreis
1968   Excavations in the Mill Creek Sites. *Journal of the Iowa Archeological Society* 15:35–106.

Kvamme, Kenneth L.
2010   Results on Geophysical Surveys at the Kimball Site (13PM4). In *Cultural Resources of the Loess Hills: A Focus Study to Determine National Significance of Selected Archaeological Cultural Resources along the Loess Hills National Scenic Byway*, ed. Melody K. Pope, Joseph A. Tiffany, Angela R. Collins, and Michael J. Perry, 4-1–4-22. Contract Completion Report 1700. Office of the State Archaeologist, University of Iowa, Iowa City.

Orr, Ellison
1942   *Report of an Archaeological Survey of the Broken Kettle and Kimball Pre-Historic Indian Refuse-Mound Village Sites, 1939.* Iowa Archaeological Reports.

Titcomb, Jason M.
2012   Long-Nosed God Mask Discovered. *Northwest Chapter of the Iowa Archeological Society Newsletter* 60(1): 5–6.

Whittaker, William E.
2010   Archaeological Investigations of the Kimball Village Site, 13PM4, Plymouth County, Iowa. In *Cultural Resources of the Loess Hills: A Focus Study to Determine National Significance of Selected Archaeological Cultural Resources along the Loess Hills National Scenic Byway*, ed. Melody K. Pope, Joseph A. Tiffany, Angela R. Collins, and Michael J. Perry, 3-1–3-40. Contract Completion Report 1700. Office of the State Archaeologist, University of Iowa, Iowa City.

4 The Cowan Site and the Origins of the Middle Missouri Tradition

✳ Sioux City, Woodbury County

✳ Late Prehistoric

✳ SITE NUMBER 13WD88

BEGINNING ABOUT A.D. 1000, a new type of site appeared throughout the northern tallgrass prairie regions, an area that includes eastern South Dakota, eastern Nebraska, southwest Minnesota, and most of Iowa (see the West Des Moines Burial site [21]). It is during this time period that many aspects of historic Plains Indian life emerged: rectangular earthlodge houses clustered in hamlets, intensive maize farming, trade connections with Mississippian cultures to the southeast, as well as artifact types such as large globular pots and small notched arrowheads. Archaeologists call one early manifestation of Plains village life Great Oasis, and it was most common in western and central Iowa.

Great Oasis was short-lived, lasting only a couple centuries, but it appears to be the direct ancestor of the subsequent Initial Middle Missouri (IMM) tradition, aspects of which existed well into the historic period and were familiar to early European explorers along the Missouri River. Great Oasis sites represent a transition from the Late Woodland to the Late Prehistoric, sharing aspects of both. Like the Late Woodland, Great Oasis sites show a mix of wild and domestic plants, with perhaps a greater reliance on maize farming. As in the Late Woodland period, evidence for houses is rare at excavated sites: we know of only six houses from three Iowa sites. In contrast, in the subsequent IMM tradition, houses are common. All known Great Oasis houses are rectangular, like those of the later IMM tradition. Unlike IMM sites, however, Great Oasis sites are never fortified with ditches or embankments. The pottery archaeologists have recovered closely resembles that from IMM sites, and people in both periods dug bell-shaped storage pits.

The Cowan site at the northeast edge of Sioux City is a classic example of Great Oasis and is probably the most intensively excavated site from this

Artist's drawing of a Great Oasis house. Artist unknown.

period. When archaeologists investigated this site in 1995 and 1998 prior to the construction of a highway, they did not find direct evidence of houses, but they inferred the location of three based on artifact and feature distribution. The intensive excavation and exhaustive analysis of the Cowan site allowed new inferences to be made about the people who lived during these years. While the Cowan inhabitants grew lots of maize, they also relied very heavily on animals and wild plants, including deer, bison, dog, goosefoot, amaranth, maygrass, and sunflower. There was little evidence of long-distance trade, other than shell beads from the Mississippi valley and small amounts of cherts from the western Plains and the Mississippi valley. By analyzing the pot rims they found, the researchers estimated that at least 558 vessels existed at the site. The projected size of the houses led to an estimate that about 18 to 31 people lived at Cowan, and combining that number with the number of pots a person could be expected to use per year, archaeologists estimated that the site was occupied for about 3.8 to 9.5 years. They also recovered bones from seven individuals in different contexts, including possible storage pits, but these remains were so fragmentary that no real conclusion about burial practices was possible.

Perhaps the greatest legacy of Cowan is that its excavation allowed for a critical revaluation of Great Oasis. Stephen Lensink and Joseph Tiffany carefully combed through all known data from every suspected Great Oasis

Excavating storage pits at the Cowan site, 1988, Woodbury County.

site and compiled detailed lists of excavations and results. They were able to refine the age and spatial extent of Great Oasis and offer insights about its origin and relationship to contemporary cultures.

✳ TO VISIT

The Cowan site is located near the intersection of U.S. Highway 75 and 46th Street in northeast Sioux City. The Sioux City Public Museum, 607 4th Street, Sioux City (712-279-6174), has displays of artifacts from excavations and collections of the region, and currently has a long-term display of artifacts from the Cowan site.

✳ WANT TO LEARN MORE?

Doershuk, John F., and Toby A. Morrow
1999   The Cowan Site: A Great Oasis Component in Northwest Iowa. *Newsletter of the Iowa Archeological Society* 49(1): 3–4.

Lensink, Stephen C., and Joseph A. Tiffany, eds.
2005   *The Cowan Site: A Great Oasis Community in Northwest Iowa.* Report 22. Office of the State Archaeologist, University of Iowa, Iowa City.

5 Sergeant Floyd's Grave—America's First National Monument

❋ Woodbury County

❋ Historic (1804)

❋ SITE NUMBER 13WD184

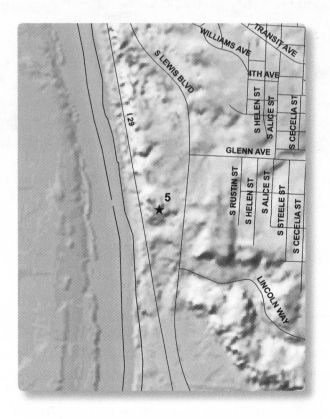

IN 1804, MOST OF WHAT is now Iowa was terra incognita to Americans. The United States had acquired the region in 1803 as part of the Louisiana Purchase; lands west of the Mississippi valley were largely blank on American maps. The valley itself was an established part of European trading networks, so Americans were familiar with the geography, Indian tribes, and political climate of eastern Iowa. The peoples of what would become central and western Iowa, however, had very little direct contact with the United States, and when Zebulon Pike surveyed the lower Des

Floyd Monument, 2014,
Woodbury County. Photo
by Jon C. Nylen. Courtesy
of Nylen Photography, Inc.

Moines River in 1805, he gave only the barest sketches of the interior of the
future state. More information came from Lewis and Clark's expedition,
which explored the Missouri River in 1804, meeting with tribes, mapping
the river, and even documenting an Ioway village in southwest Iowa—
already abandoned when the Corps of Discovery passed through the area.

The expedition also left behind one of its members in Iowa, the only one
to die during the journey. Sergeant Charles Floyd, of Kentucky, began to
feel pain in his stomach in late July, as the party went up the Missouri along
what is now Iowa. It is not clear what his ailment was, but a reasonable
guess is appendicitis. On August 20, Floyd died, probably of peritonitis.
His comrades held a funeral and buried him on a high bluff overlooking
the Missouri River south of what is now Sioux City, marking his grave with
a large cedar post carved "Sergt. C. Floyd died here 20th of August 1804."
Clark wrote in his journal: "We buried him on the top of the bluff a Mile

below a Small river to which we Gave his name, he was buried with the Honors of War, much lamented."

In 1832, George Catlin painted his grave and its surroundings. Cattle grazed on the bluff, and eventually overgrazing and cow trails caused the edge to become unstable. By 1857, erosion degraded the bluff to the point that Floyd's bones were exposed. He was reburied a few hundred yards to the east. After the publication of his journal in 1894, Iowans took newfound pride in their adopted son and buried him a third time with a new marker. In 1900, citizens built a 100-feet-tall white Kettle River sandstone obelisk monument nearby and buried his bones for a fourth time. Thousands attended a grand ceremony, held on Memorial Day, May 30, 1901, to rededicate Floyd's gravesite.

It was only because of Floyd's fame that his gravesite was preserved. Most historical sites were not so fortunate because until the 1960s there was no sustained federal effort to protect historic locations. Floyd's monument became the nation's first National Historic Landmark on June 30, 1960, because of his association with the Lewis and Clark expedition and the architecture of the obelisk memorial.

✴ TO VISIT

From Sioux City, take Old Highway 75 south of town. Look for the large obelisk. The Sergeant Floyd River Museum and Welcome Center is nearby at 1000 Larsen Park Road (712-279-0198), www.siouxcitymuseum.org.

✴ WANT TO LEARN MORE?

Annals of Iowa
1901   Dedication of the Floyd Monument. *Annals of Iowa* 5:148–149.

National Park Service
2004   *Lewis and Clark Expedition: Sergeant Floyd Monument.* http://www.nps .gov/nr/travel/lewisandclark/ser.htm.

Sioux City Public Museum
2013   *Sioux City History: Floyd Monument.* www.siouxcityhistory.org /historic-sites/102-sergeant-floyd-monument.

6 Double Ditch: Uncovering a 12th-Century Iowa Community with 21st-Century Technology

＊ *O'Brien County*

＊ *Late Prehistoric*

＊ SITE NUMBER 13OB8

ABOUT THE TIME the Incas rose to dominate the South American Andes and the Normans invaded England, Native Americans established a small village overlooking a tranquil valley in today's O'Brien County, Iowa. Timber along the creek provided the raw material for perhaps 10–12 rectangular-shaped timber and plaster-walled lodges, banked or covered with earth, and grouped closely together. The position of this small village along the terrace edge offered a long view of the valley's resources and afforded a vantage point to monitor approaching strangers — friend or foe. Grassy, circular dips on the site's surface today denote the location of former houses, and linear depressions outline two 8-feet-wide ditches surrounding the settlement. The ditches may have fronted a timber stockade, created to frustrate anyone threatening to raid the caches of dried food stored beneath the house floors. Almost a millennium later, archaeologists would name the site "Double Ditch" after these most distinguishing features.

Decades of archaeological research tell us that the Double Ditch site represents the northernmost of some three dozen similar villages found along the Little Sioux and Big Sioux Rivers and their tributaries in northwest Iowa. The Kimball (3) and Wittrock villages (8) are two others. All belong to the Mill Creek culture first described and named by Charles R. Keyes decades ago, and later classified by archaeologists as belonging to the Initial Middle Missouri (IMM) tradition (see the Cowan site [4]).

Until recently, archaeological studies provided a fairly complete picture of life in a Mill Creek community. We know that villages date to A.D. 1100–1250 and share similar house types, with structures often arranged in regular streetlike fashion, surrounded by a ditch and wooden palisade. The

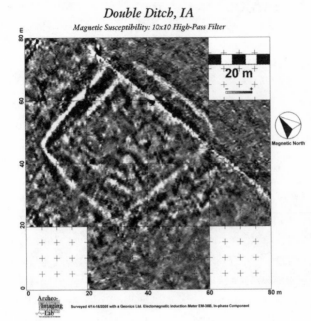

Double Ditch, IA
Magnetic Susceptibility: 10x10 High-Pass Filter

Double Ditch site, O'Brien County. Map of site resulting from magnetic susceptibility survey shows outline of surrounding ditches and house locations. Created by ArchaeoImaging Lab, University of Arkansas.

residents hunted bison, elk, and deer with bows and arrows; fished using bone hooks; and gathered many types of plants. They were also the first big-time corn farmers in Iowa—a lifestyle that required permanent communities to plant, maintain, harvest, and store surplus crops. Because people were living year-round in one spot for several decades, they created stunning quantities of distinctive stone, pottery, shell, and bone artifacts. Among these are items Mill Creek people acquired from as far away as the Gulf Coast, probably via trade through Mississippian towns such as Cahokia near modern-day St. Louis.

While grazed pasture covers and preserves most of the Double Ditch village, approximately one-quarter of the site has been disturbed by modern plowing. All surface clues to the surrounding ditches or house depressions in this portion of the site are gone. Geophysical survey helped fill in the rest of the story, and the settlement.

Geophysical survey uses a variety of nondestructive sensing technologies to detect and map buried archaeological features. The OSA, with the help of volunteers from the Iowa Archeological Society, enlisted the services of the University of Arkansas to study Double Ditch using four geophysical survey techniques: electrical resistance, conductivity, magnetic gradiometry, and magnetic susceptibility. All of these techniques measure the contrast between archaeological remains at a site and the surrounding soil. Such remains include features made by humans, such as walls, ditches, pits, and house floors. The combined results at Double Ditch created a stunning overview of the village layout. The perimeter ditches in both the plowed and unplowed portions of the site could now be seen, along with evidence of several new lodges as well as the precise location of their front entryways.

The results at Double Ditch for the first time demonstrated the value of applying geophysical survey to the study of complex village sites in Iowa. What was once thought lost or only discernible with extensive excavation can now be detected in a rapid, nondestructive way.

✳ TO VISIT

The Double Ditch site is near the town of Sutherland. The site is on private land, and the owners do not allow general access. To view the environs, follow County Road M12 north from Sutherland, and travel east on any of the county roads that cross Waterman Creek. Or visit the nearby Wittrock Indian Village State Preserve (8).

To see interpretive displays of Mill Creek artifacts and exhibits, visit the Sanford Museum and Planetarium, 117 E Willow Street, Cherokee, www.sanfordmuseum.org, or the Prairie Heritage Center, 4931 Yellow Avenue, Peterson, www.prairieheritagecenter.org.

Double Ditch and other Mill Creek sites along the Little Sioux and its tributaries are within the area encompassed by the Glacial Trail Scenic Byway, which offers a genuine sense of the picturesque landscape Mill Creek peoples chose to settle: www.iowalakesrcd.org/GlacialTrailScenicByway.

✳ WANT TO LEARN MORE?

Goodmaster, Christopher
2007 Geophysical Survey of a Prehistoric Fortified Village. *Newsletter of the Iowa Archeological Society* 57(2): 1–3.

2007   Multi-sensor Geophysical Investigations at Double Ditch
        (13OB8): A Non-invasive Study of a Late Prehistoric Village Site
        in Northwestern Iowa. Master's thesis, University of Arkansas,
        Fayetteville.

Lensink, Stephen C., and Lynn M. Alex
2001   Ultra-High Resolution Topographic Mapping of a Briefly Occupied
        Initial Variant Site in Northwest Iowa. *Newsletter of the Iowa
        Archeological Society* 51(1): 5–7.

7 The Litka Ridged Field Site: One of a Kind in Iowa

✳ *O'Brien County*

✳ *Late Prehistoric*

✳ SITE NUMBER 130B31

FLYING LOW OVER THE Waterman Creek valley southwest of the Double Ditch site (6) affords a bird's-eye view of an unplowed pasture covered with a series of broad, lumpy-looking ridges. The property owner often cursed this washboard topography whenever he drove over it to check on his cattle. Never did he suspect that these low earthen ridges are unique to Iowa and reveal the sophisticated agriculture of its prehistoric peoples. In fact, he had often considered leveling them.

European traders and early settlers described seeing large agricultural fields created by Indian peoples throughout the Midwest. At the early 19th-century Sauk village near Rock Island, Illinois, thousands of acres were cultivated. In contrast to the stereotypical view of small plots of maize, beans, and squash, these fields were often expansive affairs, sometimes raised incrementally above the surrounding landscape with crops planted in parallel ridges and individual hills that stretched for acres. By adding soil annually to their fields, early farmers buttressed maize roots, maintained soil fertility, and retarded weeds, pests, and diseases. Surplus crops not stored and consumed by the community were traded, initially to other villages or more nomadic groups, and later to Euroamericans.

Only a handful of raised field sites are reported in Iowa, even though ample evidence exists for intense corn farming starting around a millennium ago. Charred corn kernels and cobs, deep storage pits, and bone hoes characterize the earliest, permanent villages. In the 1920s, Charles R. Keyes (see Weed Park Mounds [62]) photographed and described a ridged field measuring 80 × 120 feet at Indian Lake, an oxbow of the Cedar River in Blackhawk County (see Black Medicine site [32]). He also referenced corn hills on Muscatine Island in southeastern Iowa. Recent lidar mapping (see Glenwood Archaeological State Preserve [13]) in Allamakee County (see

Aerial photo of Litka ridged field site with garden ridges center, O'Brien County.
Photo by Mary Helgevold.

Hewitt-Olmsted Trading Post [51]) revealed agricultural fields associated with the Ho-Chunk (Winnebago) living near Fort Atkinson in the 1840s. And below the Double Ditch site, small mounds, possibly remnant corn hills, are scattered across the Waterman Creek floodplain. It seems likely that remnants of other early raised fields were destroyed by modern plows or lie buried beneath floodplain soils.

First noted in 1985 by the Northwest Chapter of the Iowa Archeological Society and Iowa's future State Archaeologist, Duane Anderson, the Litka site consists of a series of approximately 15 linear ridges running east-west across a gently sloping terrace above Waterman Creek. The ridges today are about 80 feet long and between 3 to 6 feet wide. Of modest height (4–5 inches), each is separated by a shallow ditch measuring 6 feet or more in width. The entire complex of ridges and ditches is enclosed within an area of about 5 acres. To the south, Litka abuts the Lange site, a Mill Creek village, and it is close to the Mill Creek Double Ditch site, suggesting it belonged to this northwest Iowa culture.

In the 1990s, archaeologists from the OSA and the University of Wisconsin, assisted by volunteers from the Iowa Archeological Society, conducted test excavations at the Litka site and created a topographic map using an electronic total station transit.

Analysis and comparison of the site's soils with soils from an off-site location helped to confirm it was an agricultural field. The position of the Litka site in an upland setting, not on a floodplain, shows that its Native inhabitants broke the tough prairie sod for cultivation. William Gartner, from the University of Wisconsin, who undertook the analysis of the Litka ridged fields, suggests that by planting their crops on mounded-up ridges, Mill Creek farmers improved cultivating conditions in multiple ways. The mounded soil slowed erosion and provided water storage. Mounding mixed soils from the ditches, and burned crop residue aided soil fertilization. Ridging and cropping also lessened the impacts of pests, diseases, and weeds.

Mapping with the electronic total station, the archaeologists took 6,000 measurements at 3-foot intervals across the Litka site. The resulting high-resolution map captured the site's subtle swell-and-swale topography, revealing completely unexpected details. In addition to parallel ridges, the site is a mosaic of field types, including wide flats or blocks, smaller garden plots, and shorter parallel ridges at right angles to one another. A raised enclosure borders the entire complex, and individual plots may be separated by narrow paths. Plains Indians of the 19th century like the Hidatsa describe similar fields, with gardens owned by individual women and crops planted in a way that retarded cross pollination.

The discovery of typical Mill Creek pottery within the Litka site further verified it as a Mill Creek garden. Either the nearby Lange site or Double Ditch communities, or both, could have created Litka.

To date, the Litka site remains the only documented site of its kind in Iowa or anywhere on the eastern Plains. Its complexity reveals that Mill Creek people were experienced farmers who minimized risk to their harvest by preparing their gardens to control erosion, soil moisture, and fertilization.

✳ TO VISIT

The Litka site is on private land, and the owners do not allow access. Like the Double Ditch site, you can tour the general area along County Road M12 north from Sutherland, and travel east along Waterman Creek or visit the nearby Wittrock Indian Village State Preserve (8). To see interpretive displays of Mill Creek artifacts and exhibits, visit the Sanford Museum and Planetarium, 117 E Willow Street, Cherokee, www.sanfordmuseum.org; or the Prairie Heritage Center, 4931 Yellow Avenue, Peterson, www.prairie heritagecenter.org.

✳ WANT TO LEARN MORE?

Alex, Lynn M., and Stephen C. Lensink
1996   Lange Mill Creek Site Field Work Summarized. *Newsletter of the Iowa Archeological Society* 46(4): 4–5.

Billeck, William T., ed.
1986   Garden Beds in Black Hawk County. *Newsletter of the Iowa Archeological Society* 36(4): 56.

Gartner, William G.
2003   *Raised Field Landscapes of Native North America*. Ph.D. diss., University of Wisconsin–Madison. Ann Arbor, MI: University Microfilms.

Lensink, Stephen C., and Lynn M. Alex
2001   Ultra-High Resolution Topographic Mapping of a Briefly Occupied Initial Variant Site in Northwest Iowa. *Newsletter of the Iowa Archeological Society* 51(1): 5–7.

8 Wittrock Indian Village: Quintessential Mill Creek

※ *O'Brien County*

※ *Late Prehistoric*

※ SITE NUMBER 13OB4

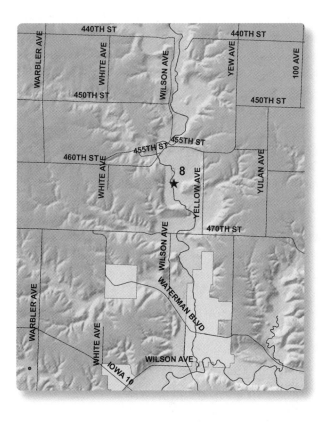

LATE PREHISTORIC Mill Creek villages in northwest Iowa have fascinated archaeologists since antiquarians discovered them in the late 1800s. For almost 150 years, local residents and professionals explored these large sites rich with artifacts, deep middens, house floors, cache pits, and hearths. These were the first compact "towns" in Iowa, and they hold important keys to understanding the nature of early Native American settlement and corn farming nearly 1,000 years ago.

Aerial photo of Wittrock Indian Village. Village outline, center of photo to left of creek.

More than 48 Mill Creek sites are known, clustered in two groups. One cluster is centered on the Big Sioux River and its tributaries near Sioux City (see the Kimball site [3]), the other along the Little Sioux River and its feeder streams closer to Cherokee (see the Litka [7] and Double Ditch [6] sites). Mill Creek residents situated their villages on river or creek terraces, avoiding broad, flat, treeless valleys, such as the Floyd River valley. These communities probably arose from local, resident Late Woodland societies, including Great Oasis, by A.D. 1100. Archaeologists classify them within the Initial Middle Missouri (IMM) tradition (see Cowan [4]).

Sites are typically compact villages with timber and earthen houses, tightly arranged in rows, sometimes surrounded by ditches and wooden palisades. Their inhabitants subsisted on the hunt—bison, deer, and elk—and harvests of corn, beans, and squash, with wild plants and smaller animals complementing the diet. Deep cache pits below house floors stockpiled dried food. Thick middens, the accumulation of village detritus and the remains of collapsed and abandoned houses, characterize some sites. Known burial locations—cemeteries and ossuaries—occur nearby, with occasional interments found within houses or middens. Excavations produce prodigious quantities of ground and chipped stone tools, ceramics, bone and shell implements, items of personal adornment, fire-cracked rock, butchered animal bone, and burned seeds and charcoal—a material culture befitting a year-round "metropolitan" lifestyle. From some sites, exotic materials such as marine shell and pottery, foreign to northwest Iowa, offer convincing evidence that Mill Creek people made contacts through trade and travel with distant cultures.

The Wittrock site, immediately adjacent to the left bank of Waterman Creek on a flat terrace about 4 miles downstream from the Litka and Double Ditch sites, remains the "model" for this depiction of Mill Creek life. Apart from archaeological study, Wittrock has not been impacted by construction or cultivation. From the air, even today, the site pops out as a dense mass of vegetation embedded with the outlines of a rectangular ditch surrounding almost two dozen lodge depressions. Acquired in 1937 by the Iowa Conservation Commission, Wittrock is a National Historic Landmark and was dedicated a state preserve in 1968—a charter member of Iowa's new State Preserve System (see Woodland Mounds State Preserve [25]).

Archaeologists undertook four excavations at Wittrock. In 1959, Reynold J. Ruppé, from the University of Iowa, excavated a narrow test trench across the ditch and into the village, and dug a large portion of one of the house depressions. Four years later, the University of Wisconsin conducted modest excavations in the site's midden deposits as part of a broader study to determine the effect of climate change on Mill Creek culture. In 1965, Marshall McKusick's extensive excavations for the University of Iowa delineated the site's settlement pattern. He uncovered uniformly sized and arranged semisubterranean rectangular lodges with south-facing entryways. Evidence for a perimeter defense consisted of a 7-feet-wide ditch, an interior timber stockade with bastions, and several earthen causeways that crossed into the village. Embankments on either side of the ditch amplified its steep drop to nearly 10 feet—a formidable obstacle for any uninvited callers. Central hearths and cache pits dotted the house floors and produced the characteristic array of Mill Creek items and discards. In 1980, Anthony Zalucha, of the University of Wisconsin, returned to the site to conduct limited testing to acquire data for paleobotanical reconstructions.

The collective research at Wittrock indicates the site was late (perhaps post A.D. 1200) in Mill Creek history but with two possible periods of occupation. People lived here for shorter episodes than previously thought, the site growing in depth probably as a result of the accumulation of debris and soil used to bank the exterior walls of houses. Subsistence data demonstrates the inhabitants' preference for bison, but whether the abundance of this animal was due to climatic, ecological, or cultural factors is unknown. Wittrock showed little evidence for long-distance trade, a conclusion reinforced by a recent chemical analysis of five pipestone artifacts from the site, which demonstrated their manufacture from pipestone found in local river gravels.

Since the 1980s, attention to the site as a state preserve has focused on management and interpretation. Control structures were built to protect the western edge from erosion, and a partial stockade with bastions was reconstructed to provide visitors a sense of what they might have seen had they stopped by 800 years ago.

✳ TO VISIT

The Wittrock site is northeast of Sutherland. As the Wittrock Indian Village State Preserve, the site is state-owned and managed by the O'Brien County Conservation Department. Access is by permission across private land or via boat down Waterman Creek. Contact the Iowa Department of Natural Resources: www.iowadnr.gov/Destinations/StatePreserve.

To see interpretive displays of Mill Creek artifacts and exhibits, visit the Sanford Museum and Planetarium, 117 E Willow Street, Cherokee, www .sanfordmuseum.org; or the Prairie Heritage Center, 4931 Yellow Avenue, Peterson, www.prairieheritagecenter.org. Wittrock and other Mill Creek sites along the Little Sioux and its tributaries are within the area encompassed by the Glacial Trail Scenic Byway, which offers a genuine sense of the picturesque landscape Mill Creek peoples chose to settle: http://www .iowalakesrcd.org/GlacialTrailScenicByway.htm.

✳ WANT TO LEARN MORE?

Anderson, Duane C.
1985 *Excavations at the Wittrock Site (13OB4): A Compilation of Information Pertaining to Projects Conducted in 1959 and 1965.* Research Papers 10(1). Office of the State Archaeologist, University of Iowa, Iowa City.

1986   The Wittrock Excavations: Implications for the Study of Culture Process within the Initial Variant of the Middle Missouri Tradition. *North American Archaeologist* 7:215–241.

Gundersen, James N., and Joseph A. Tiffany
1986   Nature and Provenance of Red Pipestone from the Wittrock Site (13OB4), Northwest Iowa. *North American Archaeologist* 7:45–67.

Henning, Dale R., Amy E. Harvey, and David A. Baerreis
1968   Excavations in the Mill Creek Sites. In *Climatic Change and the Mill Creek Culture of Iowa*, Part 1, ed. D. R. Henning. *Journal of the Iowa Archeological Society* 15:35–106.

Herzberg, Ruth, and John Pearson
2001   *The Guide to Iowa's State Preserves.* Iowa City: University of Iowa Press.

Tiffany, Joseph A.
2007   Examining the Origins of the Middle Missouri Tradition. In *Plains Village Archaeology: Bison-Hunting Farmers in the Central and Northern Plains*, ed. Stanley Ahler and Marvin Kay, 3–14. Salt Lake City: University of Utah Press.

9 Ancient Bison Hunting at the Cherokee Sewer Site

* Cherokee, Cherokee County
* Archaic
* SITE NUMBER 13CK405

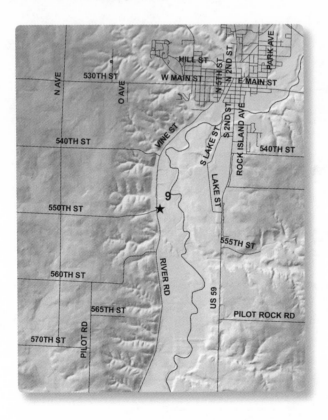

BISON ARE animals of habit. They tend to follow the same trails year after year, their sharp, heavy hooves cutting deep into the soil, leaving a trace that their descendants will follow for centuries. Native Americans knew well the habits of bison, and took advantage of them. For almost 2,000 years Indians hunted along a well-established bison trail south of Cherokee. At least four distinct occupations reveal changes in hunting from the Early Archaic period about 9,000 years ago to the Middle Archaic period about 7,000 years ago.

As herds crossed the valley of the Little Sioux, they often went over the west bluff through a narrow drainage; this was easier for the bison than trying to scamper up the steep bluff slope, but it also confined them to a narrow area where Indians could more easily hunt them. We don't know exactly how these ancient people killed their prey, but it required planning and skill; you just can't walk up to a bison on the prairie and stab it with a spear. Historically, Indians used a number of tricks, everything from building makeshift corrals to dressing up in wolf skins to herd the animals to a kill spot, or driving them into the edge of a muddy river. Bison jumps, where large numbers from a herd were stampeded off steep slopes, occurred in the northern high plains, but are unknown in Iowa.

In 1973 and 1976, prior to the expansion of a wastewater treatment plant, the University of Iowa excavated the Cherokee Sewer site. The dig was a cross-disciplinary effort, involving geologists, archaeologists, and paleontologists. The site was deeply buried, and the researchers used new excavation techniques for the first time in Iowa, including metric grid excavation and extensive water screening. Other innovative techniques included the use of snail, micromammal, and pollen remains to study climate change. The time period covered by the four known habitation levels coincides with

Horizon II, Square 28, showing bison bones, Cherokee Sewer site, Cherokee County.

Overview of excavations at the Cherokee Sewer site, Cherokee County.

the advent of the Hypsithermal, a period of warmer and dryer weather that caused the expansion of short-grass prairie into Iowa.

Each time the site was occupied, the Indians killed and butchered a small group of bison, from 6 to 16 at a time. Butchered bison bone and stone cutting tools found surrounding hearths at the site suggest the people sat around the campfires while they worked.

Over time, as the climate changed, bison became smaller, and the site's residents replaced the lanceolate-shaped projectile points used early on with stemmed points; site features such as pits for cooking food became more common; and hunting techniques changed. We can reconstruct hunting strategies by studying the bones and teeth of bison, which can suggest the animal's age, the season of a kill, and the butchering techniques utilized. In the first Early Archaic occupation, people hunted younger bison in the early winter. This was partly true in the second Early Archaic occupation, although the bison were no longer exclusively younger. In the last occupation, during the Middle Archaic, the hunters only pursued older bison.

✳ TO VISIT

From the town of Cherokee, follow River Road south; the site is along the south edge of the treatment plant, near the intersection of 550th Street. Artifacts from the site, including a unique bird bone flute, may be seen at the Sanford Museum and Planetarium, 117 E Willow, Cherokee, www.sanford museum.org. A good selection of artifacts and bones from the Cherokee Sewer site are also on display at Iowa Hall in the University of Iowa Museum of Natural History, Iowa City.

✳ WANT TO LEARN MORE?

Anderson, Duane C., and Holmes A. Semken Jr., eds.
1980   *The Cherokee Excavations: Holocene Ecology and Human Adaptations in Northwestern Iowa.* New York: Academic Press.

Whittaker, William E.
1998   The Cherokee Excavations Revisited: Bison Hunting on the Eastern Plains. *North American Archaeologist* 19:293–316.

Wismer, Meredith A.
2009   A New Analysis of Bison Subsistence at Cherokee Sewer, IA. Master's thesis, University of Iowa, Iowa City.

10 Dixon: Bison!

✷ Woodbury County

✷ Late Prehistoric

✷ SITE NUMBER 13WD8

BY THE 13TH and early 14th centuries, the Oneota tradition spread over much of the upper Midwest and onto the Plains (see Upper Iowa enclosures [43], McKinney [64], Des Moines [23], and Blood Run [2]). The arrival of Oneota peoples in northwestern Iowa coincided with the apparent departure of others, including Mill Creek (see Kimball [3], Litka [7], Double Ditch [6], and Wittrock [8]). In southwestern Iowa, Oneota artifacts occur in a few Glenwood culture sites (see Glenwood Archaeological State Preserve [13] and Davis-Oriole [12]), suggesting some form of cross-cultural accord before the Glenwood communities themselves were abandoned.

What drew Oneota peoples west? Archaeological investigations at the Dixon site over the past 50 years offer evidence for at least one very attractive inducement—bison.

Among the 13 known Oneota sites in northwestern Iowa, the Dixon site along the banks of the Little Sioux River is the most southerly and also the first major Oneota village known in the region. It may be one of the earliest in the state. By A.D. 1300, people were living at this large community and remained or returned here over the next century and a half. Later villages along the Little Sioux suggest a gradual relocation northward by splinter groups from Dixon or new arrivals. In the early 1700s, French maps depict Oneota descendants—the Siouan-speaking Ioway and possibly Omaha—residing near the Iowa Great Lakes and at Blood Run on the Big Sioux.

By the 1990s, archaeological studies at Dixon had disclosed the presence of a large village covering 90 acres and containing dozens of storage pits, rectangular houses, and thousands of characteristic Oneota artifacts and animal bones. These investigations, and an unfortunate amount of vandalism at the site, also demonstrated the presence of burials, not uncommon in an Oneota village. When massive flooding hit the Midwest in 1993, it

Oneota vessel from the Dixon site, Woodbury County.

destroyed or damaged many archaeological sites. At Dixon, 50 storage pits now lay exposed in the cutbank of the Little Sioux. The flood presented the opportunity, and the federal funds, for an archaeological team from the OSA to salvage additional information from Dixon.

The 1994 work at Dixon shed new light on the settlement and lifeways of its residents. Archaeologists uncovered remnants of five new structures, and portions of three were excavated—two rectangular in shape and one oval. All had an east-west orientation and had been constructed within semisubterranean basins with walls supported by a single line of wooden posts. Dozens of storage pits, some with clay caps and internal lenses of clay, dotted the floors of the rectangular houses. The clay caps likely functioned to protect the caches of stored food—especially corn (see also McKinney [64]). The clay lenses may have addressed a more unpleasant problem in the houses—sealing off the odors from rotting garbage used to fill the pits once they no longer functioned for storage. Richard Fishel, the project director, proposed that the atypical shape of the oval structure and its lack of storage pits hinted that it served a different, unknown purpose. Historic villages often had a number of specialized structures for ceremonies, councils, and personal retreats during fasting or menstruation.

Excavation of the Dixon site, view to the north, Woodbury County.

Intriguingly, the floors of all the structures excavated in 1994 produced fewer artifacts than expected, suggesting the inhabitants had swept them clean and stashed or removed their belongings before they vacated the houses. Was this because Dixon residents had taken or hidden their possessions when they left? Many later Plains tribes virtually deserted their villages for annual or semiannual bison hunts farther to the west. Could this explain the "tidy" houses at Dixon?

Large quantities of bison bone and the stone artifacts from the site demonstrated the importance of bison hunting. Chipped stone arrow points, knives, and end scrapers—tools associated with hunting, butchering, and hide processing—were common. Bison shoulder blades (often used as digging tools) and large limb bones—bones that yield the highest amount of meat, marrow, and bone grease—proved most numerous. This hinted that some hunting occurred away from the village, perhaps at times when game was depleted closer to home, and only select parts of the butchered animals were hauled back to the village. The highly fragmented condition of the bone also demonstrated that Dixon residents broke open the bone to extract the highly nutritious marrow and probably boiled it to recover bone grease.

In mapping out the source locations for the raw materials used to make chipped stone tools, it became evident that Dixon people utilized stone from a broad area of the Midwest and Plains, but especially north-central Kansas and south-central Nebraska. Pipestone found at the site also derived from Kansas sources. Contemporary Oneota sites in these regions, in turn, contain large amounts of bison bone and artifacts characteristic of hunting and processing. They also contain Dixon-style pottery.

Fishel suggests that Dixon hunters traveled up to 200 miles to participate in communal bison hunts with other Oneota peoples in central Kansas and Nebraska. Here they obtained not only the fruits of the hunt but also raw materials for stone tools. Large dogs may have served as pack animals on these excursions. Their bones were the third most common type found at the site.

✳ TO VISIT

The Dixon site, now on the National Register of Historic Places, lies on private land along the Little Sioux River near the town of Anthon in Woodbury County. Looting and erosion over the years have greatly impacted the site. To see interpretive displays of northwest Iowa Oneota, visit the Sioux City Public Museum, 607 4th Street, Sioux City (712-279-6174): www.siouxcity museum.org.

✳ WANT TO LEARN MORE?

Fishel, Richard L.

1995 *Excavations at the Dixon Site (13WD8): Correctionville Phase Oneota in Northwest Iowa.* Contract Completion Report 442. Office of the State Archaeologist, University of Iowa, Iowa City.

Fishel, Richard L., ed.

1999 *Bison Hunters of the Western Prairies: Archaeological Investigations at the Dixon Site (13WD8), Woodbury County, Iowa.* Report 21. Office of the State Archaeologist, University of Iowa, Iowa City.

Fishel, Richard L., Sarah U. Wisseman, Randall E. Hughes,
and Thomas E. Emerson
2010   Sourcing Red Pipestone Artifacts in the Little Sioux Valley of
       Northwest Iowa. *Midcontinental Journal of Archaeology* 35:167–198.

Harvey, Amy E.
1979   *Oneota Culture in Northwestern Iowa*. Report 12. Office of the State
       Archaeologist, University of Iowa, Iowa City.

11 Turin: Poodle Skirts and *Life* Magazine

❋ *Monona County*

❋ *Archaic*

❋ SITE NUMBER 13MN2

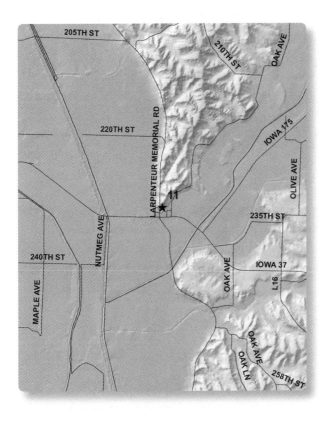

IN 1955, much to his surprise, a gravel pit operator unearthed an ancient human skeleton from the side of a steep loess bluff in the small town of Turin. Archaeologists from the Sanford Museum in Cherokee and from the University of Iowa excavated three more burials located 20 feet below the bluff top. Stone and shell artifacts found with the burials clearly identified the site as an ancient cemetery—one of the oldest found

Youngsters visiting the Turin site excavation, 1955, Monona County.

in Iowa. In fact, since the loess deposits in which one of the burials occurred originated during the last Ice Age, the archaeologists hailed the site as a late Pleistocene (Ice Age) discovery—rare anywhere in North America. Prominent archaeologists and paleontologists flocked to the scene, as did local residents and schoolgirls decked out in poodle skirts and crinolines. The discovery received national attention in *Life* magazine with a two-page spread and photographs in the September 1955 issue.

The burials included the remains of four young people, three of them probably under the age of 13, all carefully placed in a flexed position, knees drawn up to the chest. One of the youngsters had been interred in a shallow pit and sprinkled with red ocher—a custom widespread in the ancient world. Ocher derives from ground-up hematite, a common form of iron oxide. Stone spear points and shell beads—likely strung as a necklace or sewn onto clothing—accompanied him. The spear point suggested an Archaic style, rather than the Paleoindian type that might be expected if the site were Pleistocene in age.

Reinvestigation of the findings years later did in fact show that the site was not as old as originally thought. Several thousand years after the

Archaic period projectile
point, Turin site, 1955,
Monona County.

Turin site excavation, 1955.

Pleistocene loess was deposited, a gully cut through the bluff, reworking and redepositing the loess soils. The graves had actually been dug into this reworked loess. The types of land snails and seeds collected from the surrounding soils suggested a post–Ice Age environment, supporting the younger age as well. The style of the projectile point and radiocarbon dates suggested a Middle Archaic date, 5,000–6,000 years ago.

Turin still remains one of the oldest cemeteries in Iowa, but it is not alone. At contemporary sites found throughout North America, people interred their dead in similar ways, placing red ocher over the burials and leaving objects like the beads and other artifacts (see the Palace site [24]). Surprisingly, the Turin beads were made of a type of freshwater snail called *Leptoxis* found in rivers east of the Mississippi River hundreds of miles from western Iowa.

✳ TO VISIT

The town of Turin is on State Highway 75 east of Onawa. The Turin site itself, on the northeast edge of town, was destroyed by gravel quarrying. Visit the adjacent city park and signage in Turin to view the site setting and learn about the discovery.

✳ WANT TO LEARN MORE?

Fisher, Alton K., W. D. Frankforter, Joseph A. Tiffany, Shirley J. Schermer, and Duane C. Anderson
1985   Turin: A Middle Archaic Burial Site in Western Iowa. *Plains Anthropologist* 30:195–218.

Life
1955   A 15-Year Mystery Gets 9000 Years Older. *Life*, September, 59–60.

12 The Earthlodge Beneath Your Feet: Davis-Oriole

* Pony Creek Park, Mills County
* Late Prehistoric
* SITE NUMBER 13ML429

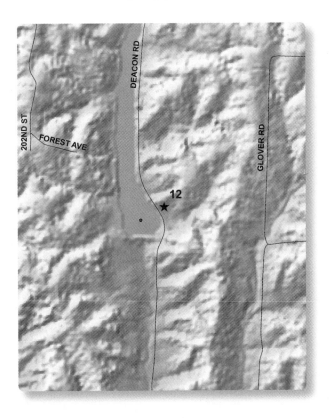

EARTHLODGES WERE THE dominant Late Prehistoric dwelling in the Great Plains. Large semisubterranean houses with timber frames and roofs and mud-plastered walls, the whole lodge possibly banked or covered with soil, these structures were well known to early explorers and traders who visited large Mandan, Hidatsa, and Arikara fortified villages filled with them. More than 300 lodges once stood in Iowa. Early European explorers, however, encountered none that were still occupied; they were probably

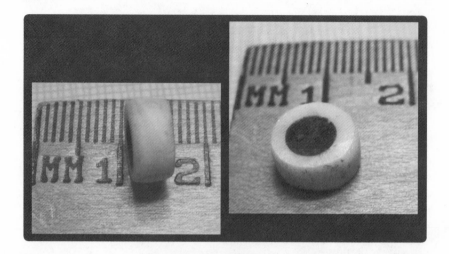

Above: Shell bead found in a Glenwood lodge at the Davis-Oriole site, 2009, Mills County.

Right: Varieties of Glenwood pottery rims: Beckman Smooth (A–E) and McVey Tool-Decorated (F).

Excavation of a Glenwood lodge at the Davis-Oriole site, 2009, Mills County.

abandoned before A.D. 1400. Archaeologists place them in the Nebraska phase of the Central Plains tradition (see Glenwood Archaeological State Preserve [13]).

Glenwood lodges generally have a square or rounded square shape, and are located on a variety of landscapes, including river bottoms, terraces, and high ridge crests. Most entryways faced southeast or southwest. The size of earthlodges can vary greatly, from 180 to 3,000 square feet, suggesting different lodges had different functions and that the number of people living in them ranged widely.

Earthlodge dwellers fished and hunted bison, deer, and small game. They gathered wild plants, but they probably grew most of their food, including corn, beans, squash, sunflowers, and gourds. Inside the lodges are the remains of hearths, activity areas, and storage pits; other storage pits are found outside. Sometimes isolated and sometimes gathered in clusters, the structures in this area probably represent small farmsteads; unlike Mill Creek lodges to the west and north (see Kimball [3], Double Ditch [6], and Wittrock [8]), Glenwood lodges were never fortified by ditches or embankments.

The vast majority of earthlodge basins in Iowa are gone, destroyed by looters, archaeologists, development, agriculture, and erosion. Recently the OSA struggled to find a fully intact lodge on public land as part of an effort to bring national recognition to the Loess Hills National Scenic Byway. One promising location was in Pony Creek Park, just northwest of Glenwood, where an amateur archaeologist, D. D. Davis, reported a possible lodge in 1991 that had not been looted or excavated, probably because it did not have a telltale surface depression.

Archaeologists attempted to find the lodge in 2008 based on the Iowa Site File map, but had no luck. It was only after carefully reviewing the original site notes that they determined the site had been mismapped and found a better location to search in 2009. The second survey found the lodge, right underneath one of the main trails in the park. Soil coring showed the lodge was approximately 40 × 26 feet. The floor of the lodge appeared to be about 35–50 inches below surface.

Now came the difficult part: demonstrating the lodge basin was intact without diminishing its integrity. In 2009, archaeologists excavated a small test unit designed to overlap the edge of the lodge and a possible hearth found in an auger test. Excavation showed a curious construction method: the lodge was dug deeper than the living floor, and then partially filled in before it was occupied. A small hearth was built on the floor in the corner of the lodge, used for heating the area or keeping a container warm, as evidenced by two Sioux quartzite cobbles that were used as hearth stones. Researchers also found a shell bead near the hearth. After abandonment, the lodge was burned, and the roof collapsed, burying the floor and turning part of the west wall daub into burned earth. A telltale potsherd, known as a McVey Tool Decorated variant, was recovered from the builder's trench, where it had likely been placed during construction. A different type of pottery, Beckman Plain, came from the fill above the occupation floor, suggesting that the people who abandoned the lodge had made and used it.

Having found an intact lodge on public land was important; it meant that the Glenwood lodges could receive national recognition through designation as a National Historic Landmark. There are only about 25 National Historic Landmarks in Iowa.

✳ TO VISIT

From Interstate 29, take exit 35, head east on U.S. 275/34 toward Glenwood. A little over a mile, turn north on Deacon Road. Head north on Deacon a little more than a mile; the park is on the east side. Circle around, park near the pond. Walk north, uphill, past the picnic shelter and to the latrine. The lodge is buried below the wide grass trail to the west of the latrine; look for the sign. To see the largest display of Nebraska phase collections from Mills County lodge sites, visit the Mills County Historical Museum, Lake Drive, Glenwood (712-527-5038). The museum is open seasonally and by appointment.

✳ WANT TO LEARN MORE?

Peterson, Cynthia L.
2011   National Historic Landmark Nomination—Davis-Oriole Lodge Site. http://www.nps.gov/history/nhl/Fall11Noms /REDACTEDDavisOriole.pdf.

Pope, Melody K., Joseph A. Tiffany, Angela R. Collins, and Michael J. Perry, eds.
2010   *Cultural Resources of the Loess Hills: A Focus Study to Determine National Significance of Selected Archaeological Cultural Resources along the Loess Hills National Scenic Byway.* Contract Completion Report 1700. Office of the State Archaeologist, University of Iowa, Iowa City.

13 Glenwood Archaeological State Preserve

* *Mills County*
* *Late Prehistoric*
* SITE NUMBER 13ML82

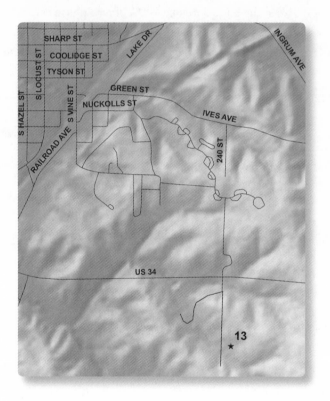

LONG BEFORE professional archaeologists set foot in southwest Iowa's unique Loess Hills, local residents, relic hunters, and antiquarians filled boxes and picture frames with collections of stone projectile points and pieces of pottery dug from prehistoric house depressions and mounds. The collections, and the knowledge of individuals such as Paul Rowe and D. D. Davis in Mills County, guided archaeologists to many sites — most of them the footprints of earth and timber lodges recognizable as depressions on the ground surface or scatters of artifacts churned up by the plow.

Subsequent investigations demonstrated that Mills County, in particular, was a favored spot for Late Prehistoric Nebraska phase farming communities. Archaeologists recorded 326 such lodges in western Iowa, extending as far south as Fremont County and as far north as Harrison County. The vast majority (308) of the lodges are close to Glenwood, near Pony and Keg Creeks in the bluffs to the east of the Missouri River, opposite the mouth of the Platte River. One study revealed that almost all lodges can be found within 10 miles of the mouth of the Platte following creek drainages.

The dedication in 2009 of the Glenwood Archaeological State Preserve, the 96th and largest archaeological preserve in the State Preserve System (see Woodland Mounds State Preserve [25]), acknowledges this exceptional archaeological legacy. The preserve land was formerly part of the Glenwood Resource Center, an institution that served Iowa's homeless and individuals with disabilities for 150 years. In the 1930s and 1940s, men from the center, then called the Iowa Institution for Feeble-Minded Children, helped excavate earthlodges on the grounds for the Smithsonian Institution and for later archaeologists. Francis McDowell, an adult hospital resident, maintained correspondence with archaeologists Paul Rowe and Ellison Orr for years, discussing his excavations and observations about the Glenwood earthlodges. As Ellison Orr described it, "this digging is one of the few bright spots in their drab lives."

Even after previous land terracing, cultivation, and the intrusion of U.S. Highway 34, the Glenwood Archaeological State Preserve's 906 acres still contain a dense concentration of archaeological sites dating from Late Paleoindian times 10,000 years ago to the pioneer era. The 600-to-800-year-old Nebraska phase sites dominate, however. Of the 133 recorded sites within the preserve, 34 are Nebraska phase sites, with at least 24 lodges or probable lodges. The Nebraska phase belongs to the Central Plains tradition, one of two major Plains traditions found in Iowa. Nebraska phase lodges were square to rectangular structures from 300 to 1,850 square feet. A pit was excavated to form the earthen floor with a hearth at its center. Timber framing supported walls of wattle and daub. Often, the entryway was sloping and extended outward as an appendage from one end of the structure. Earth and sod may have been stacked up against the walls and over the wooden roof frame to create an actual "earthlodge," but less is known of these architectural details.

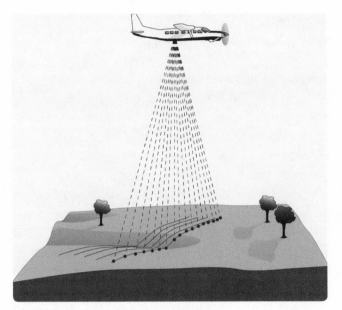

Drawing illustrating aerial lidar mapping (Angela R. Collins).

To provide a management plan for the new preserve, the OSA conducted survey, test excavations, and coring within the preserve boundaries. The results confirmed that Nebraska phase lodge sites were abundant—many still intact—and occupied a variety of landscape settings, from those deeply buried beneath the Horse Creek valley floodplain to others on terrace side slopes and the tops of ridge crests. While most sites contain only one or two lodges, there are a few instances where as many as 17 lodge structures sit relatively close to one another.

Lidar, a relatively new remote sensing technology, assisted the study. Lidar employs a device mounted on an airplane that scans the ground surface using a laser. The elevation of an object or the ground surface itself is determined by the time it takes the laser pulse to reflect back to a sensor on the plane. Like sunlight, the laser light can filter between tree branches and sometimes through leafed-out tree canopy. A GPS unit records the elevation points, and computer software connects these points, filtering out irrelevant objects to outline suspected anomalies on the ground. It is up to the archaeologist to "ground-truth" the results by field checking these anomalies to determine whether they represent actual archaeological

Excavated Glenwood house at site 13ML239 showing surrounding wall post holes, center roof support post holes, storage pits, and central fireplace, 1938, Mills County. Courtesy of the State Historical Society of Iowa, Iowa City, Charles R. Keyes Archaeological Collection, and the University of Iowa Office of the State Archaeologist.

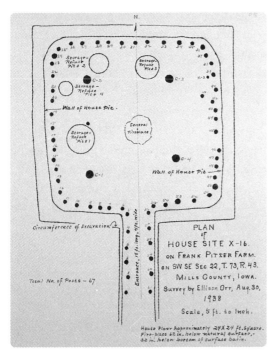

Drawing by Ellison Orr, excavated Glenwood house X16 at site 13ML239 showing surrounding wall post holes, center roof support post holes, storage pits, and central fireplace, Mills County. Courtesy of the State Historical Society of Iowa, Iowa City, Charles R. Keyes Archaeological Collection, and the University of Iowa Office of the State Archaeologist.

features—earthen mounds, ditches, enclosures, field systems, roads, and lodge depressions. Lidar detected four anomalous depressions at the preserve, later confirmed as Nebraska phase lodge sites.

The Glenwood Archaeological State Preserve protects an archive of archaeological, geological, and paleoenvironmental information. If carefully tapped, this information offers the potential to convey the story of prehistoric settlement, landscape evolution, and climate change over the past 10,000 years.

✳ TO VISIT

The Glenwood Archaeological State Preserve lies adjacent to U.S. Highway 34/275 and east of Mills County Road L45, south of the Glenwood Resource Center and the town of Glenwood. Visitors may park at Foothills Park and take the paved trail through a portion of the preserve. To see the largest display of Nebraska phase collections from Mills County lodge sites, visit the Mills County Historical Museum, Lake Drive, Glenwood (712-527-5038). The museum is open seasonally and by appointment. Visit loesshills archaeology.org for interpretive information about the preserve and the Glenwood culture. The area is also encompassed by the Loess Hills National Scenic Byway: visitloesshills.org.

✳ WANT TO LEARN MORE?

Alex, Lynn M.

2011   *The Immense Journey: Loess Hills Cultural Resources Study.* 2nd ed. Special Publication. Office of the State Archaeologist, University of Iowa, Iowa City.

Peterson, Cynthia L., Joe A. Artz, Lynn M. Alex, Melanie A. Riley, Shirley J. Schermer, Melody K. Pope, William E. Whittaker, Caitlin E. Keusch, and John L. Cordell

2012   *Archaeological Investigation of the Glenwood Archaeological State Preserve, Mills County, Iowa.* Contract Completion Report 1905. Office of the State Archaeologist, University of Iowa, Iowa City.

Thomson, Will, ed.

2013   *A Concept Plan for the Loess Hills Archaeological Interpretive Center at Glenwood, Iowa.* Iowa City, Iowa: Armadillo Arts.

Whittaker, William E.

2011   The 15-km Hypothesis for the Spatial Boundaries of Late Pre-historic Glenwood Earthlodges in Southwest Iowa. *Newsletter of the Iowa Archeological Society* 61(2): 6, 9.

14 Old Pacific City Cemetery (Kuhl Site): Equal Treatment in Death

✳ *Mills County*

✳ *Historic*

✳ SITE NUMBER 13ML126

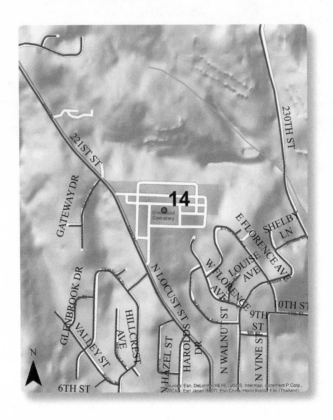

MOST 21ST-CENTURY archaeology conducted in the United States is legally mandated by federal and state laws, and much of it takes place in tandem with the construction and expansion of highways. Since 1966 and the passage of the National Historic Preservation Act, federally funded and permitted projects must take into account their effects on archaeological and historic sites that might be eligible to the National Register of Historic Places. Since the department of transportation (DOT) in each state receives federal funds and also generates projects that impinge on wide swaths of the landscape, archaeology is commonly, in effect, highway archaeology.

In the early 1970s, a pioneer cemetery in Mills County near the old abandoned town of Pacific City lay in the right-of-way of U.S. Highway 34 realignment. Some of the graves actually intruded into an earlier Nebraska phase lodge site (see the Davis-Oriole site [12]). A court order was issued to a local mortician to remove the skeletons and grave goods for reburial in a cemetery in the town of Glenwood. Instead, archaeologists from the OSA working nearby under contract with the State Highway Commission (now the Iowa DOT) convincingly argued that they could more carefully identify and remove the graves and document the lodge site than could a backhoe as planned by the mortician.

The archaeologists disinterred 27 individuals, but only 26 made it to the Glenwood cemetery. One burial contained the skeletal remains and distinctive artifacts of an American Indian woman, unofficially named the "Glenwood Princess." These were taken to the University of Iowa for analysis. Although the location and alignment of this grave with others suggested the woman was purposefully buried in the historic cemetery, Marshall

Cemetery marker commemorating Old Pacific City Cemetery (Kuhl site) reburial, Mills County.

Maria Pearson, with Governor Robert Ray (left) and John Pearson (right).
Photo courtesy of Ronald Thompson and David M. Gradwohl.

McKusick, the State Archaeologist, considered it his responsibility under Iowa law to study the remains until their historic significance could be determined.

Maria Pearson, a Yankton Dakota woman with the traditional name Running Moccasins, learned of the incident from her husband, a highway engineer. Incensed at the differential treatment afforded the Indian remains, she appealed to Iowa governor Robert Ray. Ray agreed that this was a case of discrimination, as did the public who followed the events and the war of words between Pearson and the State Archaeologist in newspaper accounts. Three months later, the remains were returned to southwest Iowa for reburial.

This incident encouraged Pearson to become an active campaigner for Indian rights and burial protection, not just within Iowa but also nationally and internationally. By the 1960s and 1970s, the practices of extracting, studying, and exhibiting ancient American Indian skeletal remains ran headlong into the objections of American Indian activists (see the West Des Moines Burial site [21]). The Pacific City incident had established a precedent in Iowa that the remains of American Indians should be treated in the same fashion as non-Indians. It would take additional conflicts in Iowa, including two major ones in the Loess Hills involving prehistoric cemeteries, scientists, and Indian activists, to propel archaeologists, the American Indian community, and state officials to collaborate in helping to resolve the burial issue.

The result was Iowa's landmark protective burial law passed in 1976, the first of its kind in the United States. The law provides for legal protection for all burials, regardless of age and whether on public or private land; reburial of ancient remains (more than 150 years in age); and statutory oversight by the OSA working with an Indian Advisory Council. Today, four cemeteries for the reburial of ancient remains exist at undisclosed locations on state lands at each of the cardinal directions — east, west, north, and south.

☀ TO VISIT

The original Pacific City cemetery site was destroyed. The burials from the cemetery were reinterred in a mass gravesite in the Glenwood Cemetery on the northwest edge of town, 1105 N Locust Street, Glenwood. A marker here commemorates the event.

☀ WANT TO LEARN MORE?

Anderson, Duane C., and Joseph A. Tiffany

2005   Beginnings: Maria Pearson and Her Role in the Formulation of Iowa's Burial Law and the Development of the Indian Advisory Committee of the Office of the State Archaeologist of Iowa. *Journal of the Iowa Archeological Society* 52:29–34.

Anderson, Duane C., Michael Finnegan, John A. Hotopp, and Alton K. Fisher

1978   The Lewis Central School Site (13PW5): A Resolution of Ideological Conflicts at an Archaic Ossuary in Western Iowa. *Plains Anthropologist* 23:183–219.

Billeck, William T.

1993   Time and Space in the Glenwood Locality: The Nebraska Phase in Western Iowa. Ph.D. diss., University of Missouri, Columbia.

Pearson, Maria D.

2005   Give Me Back My People's Bones: Repatriation and Reburial of American Indian Skeletal Remains in Iowa. *Journal of the Iowa Archeological Society* 52:7–12.

Schermer, Shirley J.

2003   Maria Pearson and the OSA Indian Advisory Council. *Newsletter of the Iowa Archeological Society* 53(3): 1–2.

15 The Hitchcock House — A Stop on the Underground Railroad

* Lewis, Cass County

* Historic (1856)

* SITE NUMBER 13CA46

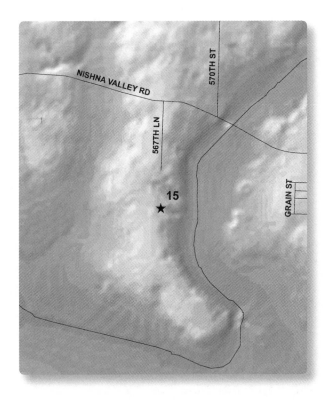

THE REV. GEORGE B. HITCHCOCK probably knew the fiery abolitionist John Brown well, and was certainly sympathetic to his cause. Hitchcock was appalled by the 1854 Kansas-Nebraska Act, which legalized slavery in Kansas and caused Brown to take up arms. Slaves escaping from Kansas were smuggled along the "Underground Railroad," and Hitchcock's house, a rectangular, two-story, reddish brown sandstone structure completed in 1856, was a major stop on the route. In his basement, a secret room

Exterior, Hitchcock House, 2003, Cass County. Photo by John Zeller. Courtesy of the State Historic Preservation Office, State Historical Society of Iowa, Des Moines.

Interior "hiding spot" in the Hitchcock House basement associated with the Underground Railroad, Cass County. Photo by John Zeller. Courtesy of the State Historic Preservation Office, State Historical Society of Iowa, Des Moines.

was hidden behind a cabinet, where escaped slaves could hide from the authorities.

The early history of the property is poorly understood; it is not known where Hitchcock built farm outbuildings or conducted other activity areas. In 2003, Steven De Vore, of the National Park Service, surveyed the Hitchcock House site with a magnetic gradiometer and an electrical resistance meter to see if he could find traces of old disturbance associated with older structures or activity areas. His work revealed large areas of disturbance, especially northeast of the house, where differences in soil properties indicated people had dug here previously. Although De Vore's work was not definitive, it does point archaeologists to areas to explore in the future.

✳ TO VISIT

The Hitchcock House is listed as a National Historic Landmark. It is located at 63788 567th Lane, just outside Lewis; it is open for tours May–September (712-769-2323). In southeast Iowa, the Lewelling House, 401 S Main Street, Salem, is another well-preserved house on the Underground Railroad, open for tours Sunday afternoons, May–September.

✳ WANT TO LEARN MORE?

De Vore, Steven L.
2003 *Geophysical Investigations at the Hitchcock House (13CA46) and Possible Cabin Location (13CA47), Cass County, Iowa.* Lincoln, NE: Midwest Archeological Center, National Park Service, U.S. Department of the Interior.

Rogers, Leah D., and Clare L. Kernek
2006 Rev. George B. Hitchcock House (a.k.a. Slave House, Underground Railway House). National Historic Landmark Nomination. Tallgrass Historians, L.C., Iowa City.

Jones, Douglas W., and Steven L. De Vore
2007 Archaeological and Geophysical Investigations at the Reverend George B. Hitchcock Properties, Cass County, Iowa. *Journal of the Iowa Archeological Society* 54:19–40.

16 Five Island Lake: What Lies Beneath?

* *Palo Alto County*
* *Paleoindian–Historic*
* SITE NUMBER 13PL89

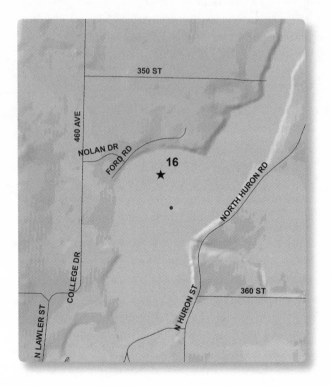

THOUSANDS OF pothole lakes, water-filled depressions formed by glacial advances during the last Ice Age, once dotted north-central Iowa's Des Moines Lobe. Prehistoric peoples found these wetlands, likely traversed more easily by canoe than on foot, to be rich sources of plant and animal resources. Euroamerican settlers thought them a nuisance to agriculture and drained 95 percent of them. One that survived is Five Island Lake, or Middle Lake, in Palo Alto County. For the last hundred years, continual

dredging of this shallow lake has sustained its use for boating and recreation. It has also created spoil piles of dumped sediment used to raise
the land surface for the town of Emmetsburg. In the late 1990s, a dredge
operator reported the discovery of fossilized bones and artifacts collected
from various spoil piles around the lakeshore.

Bear Creek Archaeology conducted a survey of Five Island Lake's perimeter and studied the dredged collections. The archaeologists identified 27
archaeological sites, including 23 located along the western margins of the
lake and on small islands, and 2 within the lakebed itself. A large collection
from one of the lakebed sites, designated 13PL89, revealed a palimpsest of
items covering the past 8,500 years of human history, from Late Paleoindian Agate Basin and Angostura spear points to early historic gunflints and
horse bones.

The number and variety of artifacts and animal bones from 13PL89 indicate that this was a location where people hunted, trapped, and caught
bison, elk, deer, wolf, raccoon, beaver, muskrat, water birds, and fish.
Five Island Lake's original water levels were shallow, only 1–4 feet in most
places. Perhaps the larger animals were coerced into the shallow deposits
at the lake edge, making it easier to dispatch them. Sandbars, still visible
when lake levels are low, likely served as game trails, as they do today. Afterward, hunters retreated to campsites on higher, drier ground to eat and
process meat, hides, and furs.

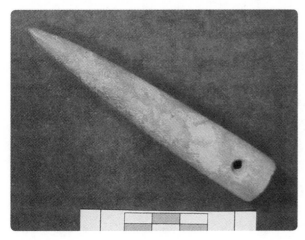

Antler artifact,
Five Island Lake site,
Palo Alto County.
Courtesy of Bear
Creek Archeology,
Inc., Cresco, Iowa.

Correlating historic maps and geological cores taken from the lakebed sediments with the distribution of recorded sites assisted the archaeologists in reconstructing the human history at Five Island Lake. The deepest lakebed sands, gravels, and clays dated to late glacial times when the lake was created. Layers of soft and hard silts, in places containing a layer of peat, were deposited over top during the past 10,000 years. These layers are the source for the artifacts; most of those from 13PL89 were peat-stained.

While sites like 13PL89 had been used as seasonal hunting camps, others found around the lake edge contained artifacts more typical of short-term processing camps. The varied and sometimes distant sources of stone from which items were made show that groups from many directions, some far away, utilized the resources at Five Island Lake seasonally, over and over again for millennia.

✳ TO VISIT

Five Island Lake lies at the north edge of Emmetsburg. Take U.S. Highway 18 to Emmetsburg. To learn more about Iowa's prairie wetlands, visit Palo Alto County's Lost Island Prairie Wetland Nature Center, 3259 355th Avenue, Ruthven: www.paccb.org/naturecenter.html.

✳ WANT TO LEARN MORE?

Benn, David W.

2000   *Shoreline Survey for Riprap at Five Island Lake, Freedom Township, Palo Alto County, Iowa.* BCA #804. Bear Creek Archeology, Cresco, Iowa. Submitted to City of Emmetsburg, Iowa.

Benn, David W., and Arthur E. Hoppin

2000   Prehistoric Artifacts from Five Island Lake. *Newsletter of the Iowa Archeological Society* 50(1): 1–4.

Stanley, David G., Deborah J. Quade, and E. Arthur Bettis III

2002   *Geoarcheological Investigations at Five Island Lake, Vernon, Emmetsburg and Freedom Townships, Palo Alto County, Iowa.* BCA #1030. Bear Creek Archeology, Cresco, Iowa.

17 Fort Dodge Military Post—
Not a Trace

⁕ Fort Dodge, Webster County

⁕ Historic (1850–1853)

⁕ SITE NUMBER 13WB509

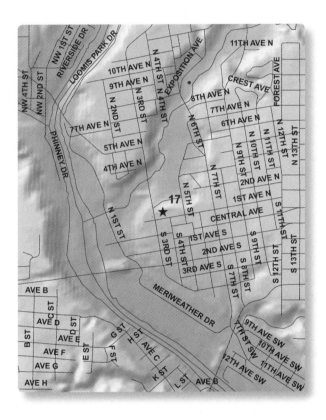

ALL INDIANS WERE supposed to be gone from Iowa by 1848, but
to the dismay of many American settlers, the Meskwaki, Dakota, Sauk,
and Ho-Chunk (Winnebago) continued to live in and visit Iowa. The Meskwaki maintained a series of small villages along the Iowa River between
Marengo and Marshalltown. The largest of these was known as "Indian-
town" and was likely the precursor of the modern Meskwaki Settlement
west of Tama. To the north and west, the Sauk still controlled north-central

View of the Fort Dodge parade grounds showing a mound or mounds in the foreground. Probably from an original sketch drawn by William Williams in 1852 and later converted to an etching for a Fort Dodge newspaper. From a copy at the Fort Museum in Fort Dodge.

and northwest Iowa, and there were several incidents that spooked settlers in the 1840s, although none resulted in violence. The Sauk and Meskwaki occasionally visited Des Moines in the 1850s.

After Fort Des Moines was abandoned in 1846 and Fort Atkinson in 1849, there was no military presence in Iowa. To better control northern Iowa during settlement, the U.S. Army established a small outpost along the Des Moines River named Fort Dodge in 1850. Never stockaded, the fort consisted of a row of buildings along the bluff overlooking Soldier Creek. From here soldiers would launch mounted patrols of the interior, and the Dakota would visit for trade, even after they ceded all lands in Iowa in an 1851 treaty. The construction of the more substantial Fort Ridgley in Minnesota in 1853 made Fort Dodge obsolete. After its abandonment, William Williams purchased the fort and made it the core of a newly planned community. In the early years, he continued to trade with the Dakota, and after the 1857 Spirit Lake Massacre (Vegors Cemetery [18]), he launched a mission to rescue survivors.

Interestingly, Williams himself made the oldest nonmap depictions of mounds in Iowa at Fort Dodge in 1852. In histories of the fort that he wrote in 1860 and 1869, he noted two Indian mounds on the parade ground; these mounds were probably shown in his crude illustrations of the fort. One

Excavations Fort Dodge, 2009, Webster County.

was excavated in 1869 and contained human remains. Utility trenching in City Square Park in the 1960s appears to have uncovered remnants of the mounds.

In 2009, archaeologists, in cooperation with local historians, began a serious effort to find remains of the fort. Armed with Williams's maps, they surveyed areas along 1st Avenue N with ground-penetrating radar, auger testing, and test unit excavation. Disappointingly, none of these efforts revealed any evidence of the fort; the landscape appeared to have been too greatly modified in the past 150 years. Archaeologists found small amounts of Woodland pottery and flaking debris, confirming a prehistoric Indian presence, but no prehistoric features. The possible mound area was not explored.

✳ TO VISIT

The Fort Museum in Fort Dodge is one of the most interesting destinations in Iowa. It contains an original cabin moved there from the fort, as well as an amazing array of artifacts from prehistoric and historic periods. The museum is located on Museum Road, just off Kenyon Road (aka Business U.S. 169 and Business U.S. 20). Most of the original Fort Dodge building was on 1st Avenue N, between 3rd Street and 5th Street. The mounds probably stood in what is now City Square Park.

✳ WANT TO LEARN MORE?

Nagel, Cindy L.

2009   Other Forts of the Dragoon Era, 1837–1859. In *Frontier Forts of Iowa: Indians, Traders, and Soldiers, 1682–1862*, ed. William E. Whittaker, 178–192. Iowa City: University of Iowa Press.

Whittaker, William E.

2009   *Searching for Historic Fort Dodge (1850–1853), 13WB509, City of Fort Dodge, Webster County, Iowa*. Contract Completion Report 1688. Office of the State Archaeologist, University of Iowa, Iowa City.

Whittaker, William E., and Alan R. Nelson

2008   The Fort Dodge Mounds: One of the First Mounds Illustrated in Iowa. *Newsletter of the Iowa Archeological Society* 58(2): 5–6.

18 Mounds, Gravestones, and Murders: Vegors Cemetery

* Webster and Humboldt Counties
* Woodland and Historic (1840s)
* SITE NUMBER 13WB76

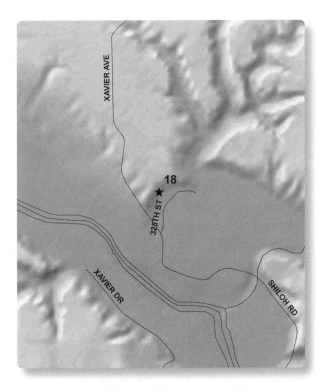

SOMETIMES PREHISTORY and history intersect in unusual ways: a 1,000-year-old mound group can help to tell the story of the chain of events that led to the last Indian uprising in Iowa.

Prehistoric Native Americans often had the same ideas about the placement of graves that the later European settlers did. Both groups often buried the dead near home; prehistoric Indians could be interred near residences, whereas settlers were often buried in family plots at the edge of

85

Vegors Cemetery, Webster County.

the farmstead. Native people often placed burial mounds on high hills and bluffs overlooking the village, just as early settlers did with their cemeteries. Sometimes prehistoric gravesites overlap later European ones. The Harpers Cemetery mound group (45) is one example, but there are several others, such as Indian Mound Cemetery, just south of Humboldt, where the east and west forks of the Des Moines River meet.

In Webster County, Vegors Cemetery overlooks the confluence of the Boone and Des Moines Rivers, with a pretty view of the fields and forests below. Here, five Indian mounds are accompanied by a few dozen gravestones, some dug into the mounds. A large obelisk memorializes Sally Lott, believed to have been the first white woman to die in the area. Her husband, Henry Lott, was notorious in his time, accused of being a horse thief and whiskey peddler. For unknown reasons, he ran afoul of Sintominaduta, a Sisseton Dakota leader. On December 16, 1846, Sintominaduta's band raided Lott's farm, burned his barn, and stole many of his possessions. Lott and some of his children either fled or were not present at the time, but his wife was left in the house, terrified. The Dakota did not attempt to harm her or her children, but the Lotts' son, Milton, ran away and died of exposure while hiding. Sally Lott suffered a nervous shock and soon succumbed to consumption, probably in early 1847. Her grave marker has several errors, including giving her husband's name incorrectly as John, giving an incorrect year of death (1849), stating that she died of exposure, and implying that she was buried at that location, whereas her exact grave location is unknown.

Seven years later, Lott found Sintominaduta and, by disguising himself, was able to befriend him. The widower then shot him in revenge. Following the shooting, Lott and his sons entered Sintominaduta's camp and killed six others, including the leader's wife and mother. These murders enraged the Dakota leader Inkpaduta, Sintominaduta's brother, who was further infuriated with the white settlers when they did not bring Lott to justice and when he heard that a settler in the village of Homer was keeping Sintominaduta's skull as a memento. In 1857, relations between the Dakota and settlers worsened after settlers in Smithland stole all the guns from a band of Dakota. Inkpaduta's fury against the injustices of the white settlers exploded, and he led the notorious Spirit Lake Massacre, in which 35 or more settlers in northwest Iowa were killed.

Also buried in Vegors Cemetery was Major Benjamin Bell, whose grave marker states that he died at the age of 102 in 1853. He is one of the very few Revolutionary War veterans buried in Iowa. Bell had migrated to Webster with his son's family in 1852; earlier he had served the U.S. Army during the Revolution as a spy on the Pennsylvania frontier, keeping a watch on Indian tribes. Other research suggests that he was not 102 when he died, but "only" 91.

☀ TO VISIT

Vegors Cemetery is located about 20 miles southwest of Webster City and 30 miles southeast of Fort Dodge. From U.S. Highway 20, head south on Stagecoach Road. In about 12 miles head west on 345th Street, turn north on Belleville Road, turn north on Shiloh/Xavier/325th Street. Cross the river; it will be the first road on the right. Indian Mound Cemetery is 2 miles south of Humboldt; follow Gotch Park Road, it is on the west side.

☀ WANT TO LEARN MORE?

Higginbottom, Daniel K.

2010   *Vegors Cemetery (13WB76), Webster Township, Webster County, Iowa*. Gone But Not Forgotten Part IV. State Historic Preservation Office, State Historical Society of Iowa, Des Moines.

19 Boone Mound: Early Public Archaeology in Iowa

* Boone County
* Woodland
* SITE NUMBER 13BN29

THROUGH THE MIST of a foggy spring morning in 1908, a railroad engineer traveling across the Des Moines River on the new Kate Shelley High Bridge west of Boone might have observed a curious scene in the valley below. A man wearing a dark suit and bowler hat directed a group of workmen who in the span of two weeks' time using horses and teams, drag sleds, and shovels would slice and dice their way through a massive 14-feet-high earthen mound, 130 × 160 feet in diameter. By 1908, this monument was already 2,000 years old.

The dapper-looking gentleman overseeing the operation was Thompson Van Hyning, curator of the Historical Department of Iowa, who, along with Edgar Harlan, its acting director, became the first state officials to plan, organize, and supervise a large archaeological project. The interest generated as word of the excavations spread to surrounding communities made it one of Iowa's earliest instances of state-supported and -funded public archaeology.

Crowds of onlookers watched from the sidelines of the excavations, some having traveled by trolley from nearby Logansport and on train from Des Moines 50 miles to the south. Hundreds followed its progress as daily updates appeared in newspapers. Guided tours at the site explained the discoveries and showcased artifacts. A professional photographer took pictures, and an engineer created a topographic map of the mound. Van Hyning wrote notes, drew profiles, and sketched plan views even as the mound fill was hauled away and plowed under.

Conducting a state-funded excavation undertaken by a state-funded institution, Van Hyning and Harlan encouraged publicity to garner continued support for the project and for the Historical Department itself. Van Hyning

Boone mound, Kate Shelley High Bridge in background, 1908, Boone County. Original photo by A. E. Moxley, Boone. Courtesy of the State Historical Society of Iowa, Des Moines.

Boone mound excavations, 1908, Boone County. Original photo by A. E. Moxley, Boone. Courtesy of the State Historical Society of Iowa, Des Moines.

even convinced local businesses to donate private funds and subsidize the trolley trips. The entire operation became a sensitive, but successful, balancing act of maintaining public interest while completing the project on time and mostly within budget.

When the excavations ceased, the mound had been completely dismantled. From its fill, the workers found modest bits of what was later identified as Middle Woodland pottery, projectile points, and fragments of human bone. At the mound base, large limestone slabs formed an irregular floor 20 × 26 feet, with additional 2-feet-high enclosing slabs set edgewise on top and partitioning off what may have been vaultlike compartments or crypts. Some human skeletal remains and ashes, possibly cremations, were found within these compartments. Van Hyning reported a depression surrounding the mound, the borrow pit for the mound itself.

Despite the Historical Department's attempts to conduct a reasonably careful, well-documented excavation, the project's scientific legacy proved minimal. Most of the artifacts, skeletal remains, and even the large limestone slabs disappeared. Van Hyning never prepared a final report, and his notes and maps, carefully copied in triplicate, apparently blew away in a Florida storm. A small collection of ceramics, stone artifacts, and mussel shell survives today at the State Historical Museum in Des Moines.

By the time the project took place, the tide of antiquarian thought was turning, and earthworks like the Boone Mound were recognized—including by Van Hyning himself—as the accomplishments of prehistoric American Indians, not mythical mound builders (see Malchow Mounds State Preserve [66]). Research adjacent to the Boone Mound in the 1960s, including a survey by David Gradwohl, of Iowa State University, confirmed the presence of a Middle Woodland settlement, the Gracie Paulson site (13BN30), likely the community whose residents had constructed and were buried beneath the Boone Mound. Analysis of the surviving skeletal remains suggested the presence of at least five individuals. Possibly one of the largest conical Iowa mounds, and one of the few known to contain such a distinctive limestone feature, the site is now known to lie at the heart of a Middle Woodland occupation in central Iowa (see Toolesboro Mounds [65]).

✳ TO VISIT

The Boone Mound site is in a private agricultural field northwest of the town of Logansport. The State Historical Museum, Des Moines, curates surviving artifacts from the site. To view the Des Moines valley landscape in the site vicinity, take a ride on the Boone and Scenic Valley Railway (www .scenic-valleyrr.com), or bike the trail across the high trestle bridge over the Des Moines River near Madrid (www.madridiowa.com/hightrestletrail).

✳ WANT TO LEARN MORE?

Donovan, Matt
2012   The Boone Mound. Manuscript on file, Office of the State Archae-ologist, University of Iowa, Iowa City.

Harlan, Edgar
1908   Boone Mound Exploration. *Annals of Iowa* 8:468–469.

Osborn, Nancy M., and David M. Gradwohl
1982   *Saylorville Stage 3 Contract Completion Report: Testing of Priority 1 Archae-ological Sites 1980–1981.* Research Report. Iowa State University Archaeological Laboratory, Ames.

Van Hyning, Thompson
1910   The Boone Mound. *Records of the Past* 9:157–162.

20 A Very Late Historical Bone Bed: The Iowa State Veterinary Carcass Pit

✳ *Ames, Story County*

✳ *Historic (early 1900s)*

✳ SITE NUMBER 13SR216

DAVID RAPSON and Matthew G. Hill, archaeologists at Iowa State University (ISU), have long been accustomed to bone beds, thick piles of the bones of bison or other animals, usually left behind by prehistoric hunters. Both have excavated numerous bone beds across the Plains and Midwest, having worked at almost every significant bison site in recent times, but neither was expecting to excavate a very unusual bone bed right on the ISU campus.

In March 2006, workers planning an expansion of the Memorial Union at ISU exposed a concentration of bone buried behind the building. News about the discovery spread quickly, and when Hill and Rapson heard about the Memorial Union finds, they persuaded ISU to delay construction while they excavated. Over 11 days a small crew worked to document every bone and artifact from one of three bone pits. Rapson led the excavations, exposing more than 1,500 bones, including the remains of 19 horses and a handful of other animals, including cow, pig, dog, cat, and chicken. The orientation of the long bones of larger animals indicated they were discarded on a hill slope. Artifacts associated with the bones included china, glassware, crockery, oil lamp parts, telephone parts, coal, slag, and electrical insulators, all suggestive of an early 20th-century deposit.

Most of the animals were pulled apart; in fact, someone had cut up their skeletons in a surprisingly consistent manner. However, the horse limbs were generally articulated, meaning they were not cut apart after being cut off the carcass. By studying tooth eruption and wear as well as bone fusion patterns, researchers established that all of the horses were older specimens, from fully adult to quite aged; many of the bones showed signs of severe arthritis. This ailment reflected not only the advanced age of the horses but also their heavy use as draft animals. Two-thirds of some tarsal bones displayed arthritis, a common ailment among draft animals. Almost none of the bones were broken, except by saw cuts and breakage caused by burial for a century. Many of the bones were partially burned, probably by a coal fire.

It was obvious early on that these bones were the remains of a dissection lab at ISU's veterinary school. Founded in 1879, the ISU veterinary school is the oldest existing veterinary school in the nation, training thousands of veterinarians to serve in Iowa and across the nation. From 1885 until 1893, veterinary school students studied at a building where the Memorial Union now stands. From 1893 until 1912, the veterinary school was based in Catt Hall; in 1912 the veterinary school expanded and built the Veterinary Quadrangle, now called Lagomarcino Hall. The veterinary college moved again in 1978, to its current facility on S 16th Street.

Among the stranger finds in the Memorial Union bone pit were bone disks of horse skulls, less than an inch in diameter with a hole in the center. These were trephination disks, the remains of bone removed with a special tool that doctors and veterinarians use to cut holes in the cranium, typically to relieve pressure. Another sign that the bone bed was the remains of a veterinary lab was the presence of vials, test tubes, corks, and lab rubber hosing. Several pieces of evidence, including the matching of horse bones from different layers of the bone bed and the types of artifacts,

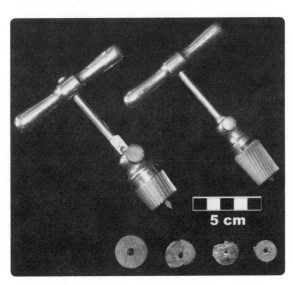

Trephination instruments and bone disks, Iowa State University veterinary school bone bed, Ames, Story County. Courtesy of Matthew G. Hill, Iowa State University.

suggest the site developed over a short period of time, probably during one school year. Looking at all the artifacts, researchers surmised that there were two sources, one stream coming from veterinary dissection labs, the other from the conversion of the old veterinary school to a carpenter's shop and storage building, reported to have occurred around 1912.

Ultimately, the 20th-century bone bed from the veterinary school proved to be remarkably different from prehistoric bison bone beds. This is not surprising: the animals were killed for different reasons — medical dissection as opposed to consumption; they were disarticulated with different tools — metal saws rather than stone blades; and they were buried for different reasons — to intentionally hide the remains rather than incidentally burying them after butchering. However, the excavation and analysis techniques were similar.

✳ TO VISIT

The veterinary school bone bed site was located at the spot of the new addition to the ISU Memorial Union, primarily where the ISU Bookstore is now located, on the lower level of the south side of the building.

✳ WANT TO LEARN MORE?

Rapson, David J., Matthew G. Hill, and George W. Beran
2007   Archaeology of an Early 20th Century Carcass Disposal Pit, Division of Veterinary Medicine, Iowa State College. Memoir 39. *Plains Anthropologist* 52, no. 204.

21 West Des Moines Burial Site

※ Des Moines, Polk County

※ Late Prehistoric

※ SITE NUMBER 13PK38

IT'S 1963. Imagine a Des Moines neighborhood with a retirement facility under construction. As the site is excavated and graded with soil hauled away for fill, human bones, potsherds, shells, and stone tools appear. Local neighborhood children and construction workers carry off human skulls and entire pottery vessels. The county sheriff and then the medical examiner arrive. They determine the discoveries are far older than their jurisdiction, and Jack W. Musgrove, curator of history from the State Historical Society of Iowa, receives a call (Musgrove is discussed in the Dee Norton site [41]). By the time he arrives, the basement for the new building is complete, and an estimated 75 percent of what had been a 1,000-year-old Great Oasis culture cemetery is destroyed.

The Great Oasis culture (A. D. 950–1100) played an important role in the development of later Plains Village cultures, especially the Mill Creek culture of northwestern Iowa (see Wittrock [8], Litka [7], Double Ditch [6], and Kimball [3]). Some 91 Great Oasis sites are concentrated in the central and northwestern parts of Iowa, with a third, smaller cluster recorded in Mills County. In northwest Iowa, sites occur near the Big Sioux and Missouri confluence (see the Cowan site [4]), and in central Iowa along the forks of the Raccoon River and the Des Moines River.

Great Oasis sites offer the first evidence that corn farming was now an important part of the prehistoric economy. Communities built small rectangular timber and plaster-walled houses with large food storage (cache) pits inside and out (see the Cowan site [4]). Animal and plant remains reflect a varied diet of hunted, fished, and gathered resources in addition to the fruits of the garden. Large cemeteries or ossuaries occur nearby. Belongings or offerings buried with the dead include shell beads created out

Spectators assisting July 1963 excavation at the West Des Moines Burial site,
Polk County. Photo courtesy of Special Collections, State Historical Society of Iowa,
Des Moines.

of freshwater snail shells from the Ohio River system and a very small number of marine shell pieces imported from the Gulf Coast—both sources
hundreds of miles from the site. These items and a few others hint that
Great Oasis peoples were extending their contacts with early Mississippian
tradition peoples of the Central and Upper Mississippi valley whose reach,
in turn, stretched far to the south and east.

Although the West Des Moines Burial site appeared to be an isolated
Great Oasis cemetery, it is likely that urban expansion had already destroyed any nearby village(s) associated with it by the time the events of
1963 unfolded.

Musgrove and his colleague, museum director Richard Boyt, arrived at
the West Des Moines Burial site on July 22, 1963, to assess the discoveries,
determine the extent of the site, and salvage any additional burials. Neither
man was a professional archaeologist, although they recorded their discoveries in notes, maps, and photographs. Even these efforts were hampered

by the circuslike atmosphere at the site, with the contractor continuing to remove earth, and dozens of gawkers standing around watching. Though cordoned off, interested spectators besieged the site, as did the press. Youngsters and others were allowed to comb through the fill dirt, and as a result additional "souvenirs" departed the site to private collections.

By July 29, when the project ended, 18 individual burials of a possible 75 original burials were removed from a burial area estimated as 60 × 70 feet in size. Later study of the skeletal remains prior to their reburial, following Iowa state law, contributed important information about the health and diet of these Great Oasis people. Most telling, perhaps, was the poor condition of their teeth; tooth decay, loss, and reabsorption were common, characteristic of individuals who have high carbohydrate foods such as corn in their diet.

The artifacts from the site revealed types and styles typical of those found at Great Oasis sites elsewhere, but Musgrove declared 33 whole and partial cross-shaped items, made of clamshell and found stacked adjacent to some burials, of Christian influence. There is absolutely no evidence for Christian contact with North American Indians at this early date, and sites elsewhere in the Midwest have cross-shaped artifacts, cross-shaped designs on pottery, and even earthworks, such as the cruciform-shaped mound at Folkert (30). The cross symbol is used worldwide, since it is both the simplest way to draw a human form and the crossing of two lines can represent the intersection of ideas or objects; in many Native American cultures a cross denotes the four sacred cardinal directions.

In 1965, the State Historical Museum in Des Moines completed an exhibit displaying five of the skeletons from the West Des Moines Burial site. The display coincided with a time of growing concern among American Indians regarding the treatment of human remains (see Old Pacific City Cemetery [14]). Outrage over the exhibit, including that voiced by local American Indian Movement (AIM) activists, reached the sympathetic ear of Iowa's governor Robert Ray. In 1972, Ray and the Board of Trustees of the Iowa Department of History and Archives directed the removal of the exhibit. Adrian Anderson, who succeeded Musgrove, supervised the reburial of the remains in 1982.

✳ TO VISIT

The West Des Moines Burial site no longer exits. Currently Crestview Acres, 9th Street and Ashworth Road, Des Moines, occupies the cemetery's former location.

✳ WANT TO LEARN MORE?

Alex, Lynn M., and Joseph A. Tiffany
2000   A Summary of the Decamp and West Des Moines Great Oasis Burial Sites in Central Iowa. *Midcontinental Journal of Archaeology* 25:313–351.

Thompson, Jerome L.
2005   We Do Not Own or Control History, We Are Merely Its Stewards–The Saga of the West Des Moines Burials. *Journal of the Iowa Archeological Society* 52:55–60.

Tiffany, Joseph A., and Lynn M. Alex
2001   *Great Oasis Archaeology: New Perspectives from the Decamp and West Des Moines Burial Sites in Central Iowa.* Memoir 33. Plains Anthropologist 46, no. 178, Part 2.

22 Terrace Hill: Garden of the Governors

＊ *Des Moines, Polk County*

＊ *Historic*

＊ SITE NUMBER 13PK53

IOWA GOVERNORS and their families have occupied Terrace Hill in downtown Des Moines since 1976, when the Hubbell family offered their stunning Second Empire–style mansion for use by the state. It has since become a National Historic Landmark. Initially constructed between 1867 and 1869 by Benjamin F. Allen, one of Iowa's wealthiest individuals, it was sold to F. M. Hubbell in 1885.

An intrinsic part of both the grandeur and the history of the property, the grounds surrounding Terrace Hill reflected popular 19th-century landscaping ideals. Both Allen and Hubbell employed landscape architects influenced by the popular English "gardenesque" school, which rejected formal structured gardens for ones that more closely imitated nature. As part of a 1970s plan to restore the property to its earlier appearance, it was necessary to determine whether any original landscaping features survived.

Archival evidence, including garden plats, family documents, newspaper articles, architectural plans, photographs, and insurance maps, hinted that early in Terrace Hill's history two possible greenhouses existed, one built during Allen's ownership, and a later one during Hubbell's. Yet as is often the case, the historic records offered murky and somewhat inexact clues as to the location, nature, and life span of these structures. Archaeological research led by Joyce McKay for the State Historical Society of Iowa in 1978 and Dale R. Henning with Luther College students in 1981 came to the rescue.

The 1978 project encountered the limestone and mortar floor of a greenhouse with an interior sand path, cistern, footings, and the post that supported a plant shelf along the sides of the building. Flowerpot fragments made up 34 percent of the cataloged artifacts. An article in the 1869 *Daily Iowa Register* indicated that Allen had constructed a "hothouse" between

Terrace Hill, governor's mansion, Des Moines, Polk County.

Historic Allen greenhouse to the south of Terrace Hill, 1880s, Des Moines, Polk County.

1867 and 1869. An 1876 legal deposition by Allen also mentions the existence of a greenhouse or conservatory on the property. Was the structure the archaeologists uncovered Allen's greenhouse, or was it a later one constructed by Hubble? A plat drawn by Hubble's landscape architect, Jacob Weidenmann, shows a greenhouse, but at a location south and west of the feature found by McKay.

Researchers from Luther College returned to Terrace Hill in 1981 to try and sort out this question, as well as to locate other garden features. Expanding McKay's excavations, the Luther College Project exposed half of the greenhouse originally discovered in 1978, allowing its dimensions to be estimated. Here they found additional internal features, including jardinière bases, post stains, concentrations of glass, pot fragments, bricks, and other refuse, as well as evidence for the heating system, which was connected to the steam-heating system for the mansion. These discoveries left little doubt that this was Allen's greenhouse of the late 1860s, one probably depicted in an undated photograph taken later. Using a steel probe to check the grounds around the excavation, the archaeologists also located pathways, walkways, stone drainage areas, and other potential landscape remains.

The Luther College team also confirmed the location of the second and later greenhouse built by Hubbell to the southwest of Allen's. This one utilized cement, a building material more typical of its later construction, and was shorter and wider than the Allen greenhouse. It was likely the one depicted on the Jacob Weidenmann plat, and in shape and size it matches a vacated structure shown on a 1901 Sanborn fire insurance map.

Archaeology at Terrace Hill assisted site restoration and preservation. Although many landscape features, including some of the garden beds, were not relocated, those that were provided important information for the restorations. The results also demonstrate the value archaeology has in clarifying a less-than-precise historical record.

✳ TO VISIT

Terrace Hill is located at 2300 Grand Avenue, Des Moines. Guided tours are available 10:30 a.m., 11:30 a.m., 12:30 p.m., and 1:30 p.m. Tuesday–Friday: www.terracehilliowa.org.

✳ WANT TO LEARN MORE?

Henning, Dale R.

1982   Archeological Investigations Terrace Hill 1981. *Newsletter of the Iowa Archeological Society* 104:1–5.

1988   Excavations of the South Lawn Area, Terrace Hill. *Journal of the Iowa Archeological Society* 35:31–39.

McKay, Joyce

1988   The Investigation of the Landscaping at Terrace Hill through Historical Archaeology. *Journal of the Iowa Archeological Society* 35:16–30.

23 Urban Archaeology in Downtown Des Moines

* Des Moines, Polk County
* Archaic–Historic
* SITE NUMBER 13PK61

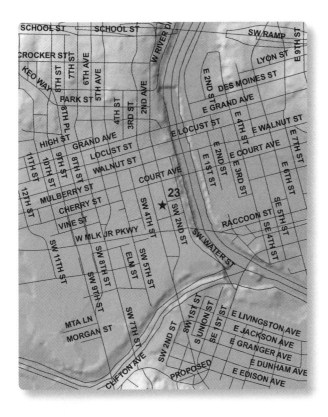

DOWNTOWN DES MOINES has always been a pivotal location; here the Raccoon River enters the Des Moines River, a merger of the two largest waterways in central Iowa. Prehistoric Indians marked this area with 15 to 18 mounds, and at least three Late Prehistoric villages stood along the west banks of the Des Moines and Raccoon Rivers.

The mounds stood on a since-buried terrace just east of the county courthouse, in an area extending from Cherry to Walnut Streets and from 3rd

Street to the courthouse. The last of these mounds was probably destroyed by 1882, engulfed by the growing city. An 1880 account describes: "Where Moore's Opera House stands [Walnut and 4th Streets] were several Indian mounds, which were about 5 feet above the surface of the soil. On the summit of one of these mounds Joseph Davis erected a house in which he lived. Another mound was where the court-house stands. There were fifteen of them on the plateau. Some of them were excavated and bones of human beings and other articles of antiquity were found. By whom they were erected is unknown. The oldest Indians found them here when they came and they had no legends concerning them."

The mounds may have been associated with three Late Prehistoric and Woodland villages that stood nearby. A village along the Raccoon, located where the Science Center is now, was occupied in the 1300s. Another village existed along the Des Moines River in the 1650s, in the park just north of Grand Avenue. A third village stood just north of Vine Street. The people who lived in these settlements were not the first inhabitants of downtown Des Moines; all three Late Prehistoric villages have older Woodland components, and an undated Archaic campsite was discovered near the Science Center under what is now W Martin Luther King Jr. (MLK) Parkway. Archaeologists discovered all of these villages in recent years, during large excavations prior to construction projects, including the Science Center, the MLK Parkway, and a large sewer.

Fort Des Moines No. 2 was occupied for a short period, 1843–1846, and oversaw the Sauk and Meskwaki as they were being forced out of the state. Early plans for the MLK Parkway led to a survey of the fort in 1982, and investigators found a fort fireplace foundation in 1985, indicating more fort features were likely, possibly under the proposed new road. Beginning in 2000, careful stripping and trenching uncovered hundreds of features, including large portions of Raccoon Row, the enlisted men's quarters, as well as the central headquarters area. Excavation of an officers' latrine revealed that these men ate a varied diet that included lots of wild plants and animals. Work on the headquarters building uncovered a wooden box built into the floor that contained floor sweepings, including military buttons and Indian trade beads. Exposure of numerous hearths and foundation remnants allowed for better alignment of the 1840s fort map with the site, so future archaeologists have a better idea where to find fort buildings.

Bird's Run site
(13PK856), 2006,
Des Moines,
Polk County.

In addition to prehistoric and fort-era features, numerous significant historic features occurred throughout downtown. Archaeologists excavated the timbers of the 1880s Walnut Street bridge 10 feet below ground, exposed the oldest paved road in Des Moines, and uncovered two fountains from the city's Beaux Arts glory days of the early 20th century.

✴ TO VISIT

Signs for Fort Des Moines No. 2 can be found at the foot of the W MLK Parkway bridge. The fort is also memorialized by a cabin that was moved there from Washington County. Raccoon Row, the enlisted men's quarters, ran along W MLK Parkway from SW 2nd to SW 4th. The headquarters was situated just east of the intersection of SW 2nd and W MLK Parkway. Officers' quarters once stood along the west side of SW 1st, from W MLK Parkway north to Vine. The oldest paved road segment in Des Moines was excavated at the northeast corner of W MLK Parkway and SW 2nd. There are no signs marking the locations of the prehistoric sites and mounds described above. Archaeologists unearthed a large fountain on the east side of the World Food Prize Building, formerly the city library; the font and much of the excavated stonework has been incorporated into the World Food Prize Building staircase on the east side. A smaller fountain was excavated just east of the YMCA.

✳ WANT TO LEARN MORE?

Dalmer, Bert
2003   Science Center Site Discoveries Are Buried. *Des Moines Register*, August 26.

Schoen, Christopher, William E. Whittaker, and Kathryn E. M. Gourley
2009   Fort Des Moines No. 2, 1843–1864. In *Frontier Forts of Iowa: Indians, Traders, and Soldiers, 1682–1862*, ed. William E. Whittaker, 161–177. Iowa City: University of Iowa Press.

Whittaker, William E.
2008   Prehistoric and Historic Indians in Downtown Des Moines. *Newsletter of the Iowa Archeological Society* 58(1): 8–10.
2012   Excavating Des Moines' First Paved Street. *Newsletter of the Iowa Archeological Society* 62(2): 2–3.

Whittaker, William E., and Cindy L. Nagel
2010   Lost Fountains: When Des Moines Aspired to Be the "City Beautiful." *Journal of the Iowa Archeological Society* 57:1–14.

24 The Palace Site: Did People Live in Basin Houses 7,000 Years Ago?

❋ *Des Moines, Polk County*

❋ *Archaic*

❋ SITE NUMBER 13PK966

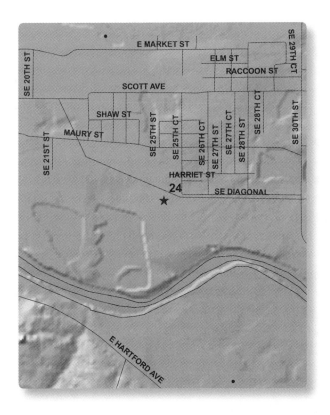

WHEN TRACTOR SCRAPERS exposed several hearths surrounded by artifacts in clay soil more than 3 feet below surface in the Des Moines River floodplain in 2010, archaeologists knew they had found something spectacular. Excavations soon uncovered five Middle Archaic occupations, the oldest human burial found in Iowa, and evidence for possibly the oldest structures known in the region.

As archaeologists hurriedly excavated and mapped artifacts and features so that a multimillion-dollar sewage treatment plant project in the city of

Excavations at the Palace site, 2010, Polk County.

Des Moines could proceed, they found several clusters of artifacts and hearths that looked like they might have been part of houses. Many of the artifact scatters took the shape of large, oval configurations with hearths in the center.

These discoveries were exciting because archaeologists previously had not seen evidence of such ancient houses in Iowa—about 6,800–7,000 years old. The Palace site resembles Middle Archaic sites of the Mississippi valley, where substantial structures often occur. It appears to be a western outlier of a trend that began 7,000–8,000 years ago when people began to settle in large river valleys and build sizable houses. Prior to this, Indians were more mobile, and there is little evidence of substantial houses.

The Palace site artifacts gave some clues about the daily life of people during this period: thousands of smashed bones and shell showed they ate deer, shellfish, fish, turtles, dogs, and other animals common in the broad Des Moines River floodplain. They gathered plants, including walnuts, acorns, and camas. Camas have a very nutritious and tasty bulb that Native

Americans used extensively. The floors of the houses appear to have been dug repeatedly, possibly when the occupants cooked the bulbs in shallow pits. The occupants used axes and other ground stone tools for woodworking and food processing, and archaeologists also found dozens of chipped stone points for knives and spears, hematite to crush into red and orange ocher paint, and cut antlers to fashion tool handles.

Faunal and floral remains indicated that people occupied the site year-round, but the quantity of artifacts and site stratigraphy suggest different houses were occupied sequentially and only for short periods. The artifacts were buried quickly, probably by annual flooding; the bone exhibits little evidence of weathering or other damage from exposure.

Additional excavation at the site using a trackhoe uncovered a human burial, an adult female with a young child. The two had been covered in ocher and buried with a few grave goods, including a spear point, hematite chunks, and a small round chert nodule. Ideally, the grave would have been left in place, but because the construction could not be modified, archaeologists carefully excavated the individuals, and they will be reburied by the Native American community.

Bison bone at the site proved scarce, just two teeth, both of which may have been from animals that died even before humans camped here. This is surprising, since all other Middle Archaic sites in central and western Iowa were almost exclusively sites where people consumed or processed bison. Furthermore, these other central and western sites do not display evidence for substantial structures or year-round occupation. Again, the Palace site more closely resembles Middle Archaic sites of the Mississippi valley.

After the site was partially excavated over the harsh winter of 2010–2011, the sewage treatment facility expansion was completed. Much of the site remains unexcavated.

✳ TO VISIT

The Palace site is located at the Des Moines wastewater treatment plant, 3000 Vandalia Road. While the facility is generally not open to the public, you can see the Palace site from the very south end of SE 25th Court at the intersection of C, B, and Q Streets. From here look southwest; the Palace site is across the railroad tracks and fence.

✳ WANT TO LEARN MORE?

Pope, Melody K., William E. Whittaker, and Angela R. Collins (editors)
2014   *The Palace Site (13PK966) A Middle Archaic Habitation and Burial Site in Des Moines.* Contract completion report 2000. Office of the State Archaeologist, University of Iowa, Iowa City.

Rieh, Nichole
2011   UI Office of the State Archaeologist Discovers 7,000-Year-Old Village in Des Moines. University of Iowa News Release. news-releases .uiowa.edu/2011/august/081811OSA_palace_site.html.

25 Woodland Mounds State Preserve: "Irreplaceable Vestiges of the Past"

❋ *Warren County*

❋ *Woodland*

❋ SITE NUMBER 13WA31

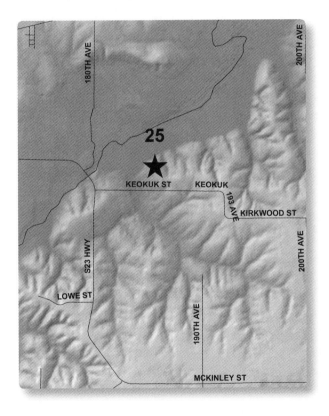

PRIVATE INDIVIDUALS own more than 98 percent of Iowa lands and the archaeological sites they contain. Many landowners are good stewards of these resources, protecting sites and assisting archaeologists with artifact discoveries and site recording. Nevertheless, like countries that recognize antiquities as part of a national cultural heritage, Iowa too realized the need to ensure protection of lands with important natural and cultural features, and in 1965 established the State Preserves System.

Two mounds beneath trees at Woodland Mounds State Preserve, Warren County.
Photo by John Pearson, Iowa Department of Natural Resources.

Properties designated as state preserves are held in public trust and receive
the highest level of protection and stewardship the state can offer. The first
10 state preserves included four dedicated for their archaeological and/or
historic significance (see Fish Farm Mounds [44], Fort Atkinson [50], Turkey River Mounds [54], and Wittrock [8]). The most recent — the Glenwood
Archaeological State Preserve (13) and new preserve near the Kimball site
(3) — were also dedicated for the archaeological sites they contain.

Most state preserves are owned by the Iowa Department of Natural Resources or the Nature Conservancy and are managed by other agencies.
The Warren County Conservation Board both owns and manages Woodland Mounds State Preserve, 195 acres of rugged, wooded uplands. Citizen-
archaeologists, beginning in the 1930s, made the first archaeological discoveries here, and their efforts ultimately brought about the creation of this
state preserve in 1983.

A group of five conical mounds inspired the property's dedication. The
mounds run north-south for over 80 feet along a prominent bluff overlooking the South River at the north end of the preserve. The largest is 121 × 85
feet in diameter, and they vary from 1 foot to over 4 feet in height. A few
small shovel excavations in the mounds' vicinity produced no artifacts or
other evidence to assist in identifying who built them or why. Based on

similar mounds found elsewhere, they are believed to be Late Woodland in age. Three parallel ridges at the south end of the group, originally identified as "finger mounds," were later interpreted as possible historic wagon ruts. Rock quarry pits found along the northernmost slope of Woodland Mounds State Preserve confirm later use of the area by settlers as a source of foundation stones.

Other state preserves dedicated for their archaeological significance include Brushy Creek, Catfish Creek (56), Fish Farm Mounds (44), Fort Atkinson (50), Hartley Fort (43), Indian Bluffs Primitive Area, Indian Fish Trap (36), Little Maquoketa River Mounds, Malchow Mounds (66), Mann Wilderness Area, Poisel Mounds (67), Slinde Mounds, Toolesboro Mounds (65), Turkey River Mounds (54), Wittrock Village (8), Woodman Hollow, Glenwood Archaeological State Preserve (13), and Spirit Knoll. Regardless of the specific resources they contain, the intent for all remains the same—to preserve, in perpetuity, "vestiges of the past that cannot be replaced or reproduced elsewhere."

✳ TO VISIT

To visit these and other preserves containing archaeological features, see Ruth Herzberg and John Pearson's *Guide to Iowa's State Preserves* (2001) and also www.iowadnr.gov/Destinations/StatePreserves.aspx.

From the intersection of State Highway 65/69 and State Highway 92 in Indianola, take State Highway 92 east for 3.5 miles to County Road S23 (165th Avenue). Turn south and go 1 mile on this winding road to Kennedy Street. Turn east and go 1.5 miles to Kirkwood Street. Turn east and go 1.75 miles to the preserve entrance on the north side of Keokuk Street and the sign "Woodland Mounds State Preserve." A parking lot is located at the end of the 0.25-mile-long entrance lane. A hiking trail, near the preserve entrance, passes the mounds.

✳ WANT TO LEARN MORE?

Conard, Rebecca

1997   *Places of Quiet Beauty: Parks, Preserves, and Environmentalism.* Iowa City: University of Iowa Press.

Finney, Fred A., Susan R. Snow, and Matthew S. Logan
1993   *Archaeological Inventory Survey and Potential of Selected Iowa State Pre-serves.* Research Papers 18, no. 3. Office of the State Archaeologist, University of Iowa, Iowa City.

Herzberg, Ruth, and John Pearson
2001   *The Guide to Iowa's State Preserves.* Iowa City: University of Iowa Press.

26 Buxton: Faces of the Past

* Monroe County
* Historic
* SITE NUMBER 13MO10

TODAY, SECTION 4 of Bluff Creek Township in Monroe County appears as a typical rural Iowa landscape of corn and soybean fields and pastures of hay. Looking a little more carefully, however, it is still possible to encounter the faint footprint of the early 20th-century community of Buxton. Here, a population of 5,000–6,000, mostly African Americans, resided in a town carefully planned and owned by the Consolidation Coal Company. In the early 1980s, the Buxton townsite became the only African American community in Iowa studied archaeologically, and an exceptional example of interdisciplinary research.

The birth of Buxton in 1900 and its demise in the early 1920s were tied to the fortunes of its creator, the Consolidation Coal Company, an affiliate of the Chicago and Northwestern Railroad. The company extracted coal from the lucrative beds of south-central Iowa to supply fuel to heat homes and run the railroad itself. Iowa was the second state west of the Mississippi to develop coal mining for commercial purposes and became the leading producer in the West until the coalfields of Colorado were developed. Buxton residents, both black and white, enjoyed steady, relatively high-wage employment as miners and mining supervisors and in essential supporting positions as doctors, dentists, pharmacists, teachers, and restaurant and store owners. With but a few exceptions, company-built churches, schools, a hotel, the large company store, and other communal establishments were integrated, as were jobs and housing.

Between 1980 and 1982, archaeologists, historians, and sociologists from Iowa State University (ISU) conducted the Buxton research, assisted by members of the Buxton, Iowa Club, Inc., an interracial organization composed of former Buxton residents. The memories, photographs, and personal correspondence shared by previous townspeople enhanced the archaeological discoveries and revealed Buxton as the vibrant community it once was.

View of Buxton, looking north from the water tower, ca. 1910, Monroe County.
Courtesy of Special Collections, State Historical Society of Iowa, Des Moines.

The Iowa State University Archaeological Laboratory crew opening up excavation
units in a former residential neighborhood of Buxton, 1981, Monroe County. Courtesy
of David M. Gradwohl, photographer.

The Buxton project was funded by a grant in support of minority and ethnic history by the Heritage, Conservation and Recreation Service, formerly part of the National Park Service. ISU archaeologists David Gradwohl and Nancy Osborn led field school students in surface survey and archaeological excavation of business, commercial, and residential districts. These studies revealed evidence for house lots, garbage pits, trash-filled cesspits, storm cellars, cisterns, wells, building foundations, gardens, streets, the railroad, a dam and reservoir, and the town cemetery. Excavations integrated with archival evidence from plat maps, photographs, and documents specifically identified many features and structural remains, including the home of the mine superintendent, the Monroe Mercantile Company store, a large company warehouse and office building, two YMCA buildings, the White House Hotel, medical offices, and the power plant.

It was, however, the personal narratives and images, remembered and recalled, offered by more than 75 Buxton residents and their descendants that personalized the scientific evidence. An excavated house lot was now revealed as the home of coal-miner Calvin Thomas; his wife, Lurena; and four children. At another property, Alice Mobilia Snead Neal, a housewife and part-time cook, raised chickens and grew vegetables alongside her irises and pansies. Her husband, George, was a renowned player for the Buxton Wonders baseball team. And Marion Carter remembered in detail the layout and contents of the office of her father, E. A. Carter, the Consolidation Coal Company physician and the first black graduate from the University of Iowa's School of Medicine.

The historical archaeology at Buxton added to the story of domestic activities, coal mining, the railroad industry, business and commercial systems, trade patterns, and urban planning in early 20th-century Iowa and the Midwest. Combined with the perspectives of former town residents, this research also demonstrated the level of cooperation, social and economic equality, and integration between African American and white populations that contrasts sharply with most other communities of the time.

With changes to both the railroad and coal mining industries, including the shift to western coal sources, and with the rise in demand for other fuel sources like oil, gas, and electricity, the Consolidation Coal Company sold its assets and in 1923 moved its offices from Buxton. This proved the death knell for the town. After leaving Buxton, many residents failed to encounter the same prosperity, equality, and integration in the communities to which they dispersed.

✳ TO VISIT

The Buxton townsite is on private land north of the town of Albia, near the Monroe-Mahaska county lines. The Monroe County Historical Society Museum, 144 A Avenue E, Albia, has an interpretive display and arranges periodic tours to the townsite. The museum is open on weekends, from the first Saturday of May to the last weekend of October or by appointment (641-932-7346 or 641-932-5085). The African American Museum of Iowa, 55 12th Avenue SE, Cedar Rapids, offers a virtual exhibit about Buxton: www .blackiowa.org/exhibits/virtual-tour/no-roads-lead-to-buxton.

✳ WANT TO LEARN MORE?

Gradwohl, David M.

2001   Investigations at the Buxton Townsite: A Coal Mining Community with a Majority Population of African Americans. *Journal of the Iowa Archeological Society* 48:95–112.

Gradwohl, David M., and Nancy Osborn

1984   *Exploring Buried Buxton: Archaeology of an Abandoned Iowa Coal Mining Town with a Large Black Population.* Ames: Iowa State University Press.

Gradwohl, David M., and Nancy Osborn Johnsen

2001   "A Kind of Heaven to Me": The Neal Family's Experience in Buxton, Iowa. In *Outside In: African American History in Iowa, 1838–2000,* ed. Bill Silag, Susan Koch-Bridgford, and Hal Chase, 2–21. Des Moines: State Historical Society of Iowa.

27 Iowaville: Village of the Ioway

* Van Buren County
* Protohistoric and Historic
* SITE NUMBER 13VB124

"HOW DO ARCHAEOLOGISTS know where to dig?" Often non-archaeologists assist them. Such was the case with Iowaville, a historic Ioway (Báxoje) village on the left bank of the Des Moines River in Van Buren County. The site area had been cultivated for decades, and local residents combed the plowed surface on foot and with metal detectors, finding hundreds of glass trade beads, gun flints, gun parts, iron axes and hoes, copper and silver jewelry, brass and copper kettles, and kettle fragments. They shared their discoveries with archaeologists, and the search was on.

The general location of the site was always known. The Ioway documented it on an 1837 map, and it appeared on even earlier maps. The Ioway, descendants of the Oneota, whose deep historical roots link them to sites such as Blood Run (2), McKinney (64), the Upper Iowa Enclosures (43), and Wanampito (31), established this village by about 1765. Possibly called "Raccoon Village" by the Ioway themselves, it was strategically located to augment their trade in furs and pelts for the selected wares of successive and sometimes overlapping French, British, and American traders who competed for their alliance.

The surface collections from Iowaville demonstrated that it contained a wealth of information about the interactions between the Ioway and the first Euroamericans in the region. At the request of the Ioway, itinerant coureurs de bois and fur company men came to the area in the late 1700s, some establishing trading posts along the Des Moines River, one just across the river from Iowaville. At least six posts dating between 1790 and 1800 extended upstream for about 20 miles, although none have been relocated. Trade company documents and church records show that French traders married Ioway women to better secure their economic toehold with the tribe.

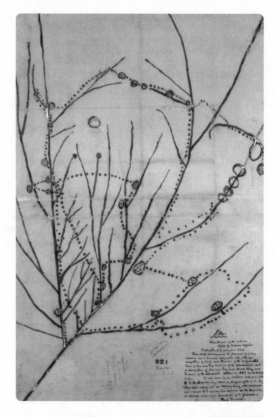

Right: Ioway map presented in Washington, D.C., 1837. Original at the National Records and Archives Administration, College Park, Maryland.

Below: Location of two circular enclosures uncovered at the Iowaville site, 2010, Van Buren County.

In 2010, archaeologists and volunteers led by Cynthia Peterson, from the OSA, and Steven De Vore, from the National Park Service's Midwest Archaeological Center, explored the site through test excavations, metal detection, soil probing, and geophysical research, including magnetic and resistance survey. The results were outstanding. The site appears to be largely intact, with surviving features such as storage pits, houses, a possible palisade enclosure, and a large circular ditch and embankment. In addition, artifacts found inside storage and trash pits reflect items made by the Ioway or secured in trade.

Dovetailing historical records and oral tradition tells us that the Ioway abandoned the village around 1820 to move west. U.S. policy now determined the political landscape on the western frontier, and the territory was soon to be opened for Euroamerican settlement. The Ioway were reduced in numbers by repeated attacks from other tribes and by the effects of major smallpox epidemics. An oft-repeated story attributing their departure to a massacre by the Sauk and Meskwaki appears to be apocryphal.

For a fleeting period in the 1830s–1840s, the Sauk also established a village to the west of Iowaville, possibly adjacent to former Ioway agricultural fields. The celebrated Sauk leader Black Hawk spent his final days near here and was buried close to the home of James Jordan, trader to the Sauk. Jordan purchased a considerable amount of land the Sauk relinquished via treaty cessions. For all of these reasons, this stretch of the Des Moines valley represents a significant "hot spot" in the contact period history between Natives and Euroamericans in Iowa.

The Iowaville site also links the past to the present in a more personal way. Treaty documents record the names of individuals who actually lived at this village, including the most famous Ioway leaders of the time—White Cloud, No Heart, and the Orator. Their descendants and other Ioway today have a profound interest in the history of Iowaville and are deeply concerned for the site's future preservation.

✳ TO VISIT

The Iowaville site is along the Des Moines River near Eldon. The site is on private land, and the owners discourage visits. The historic cemetery for the later short-lived town of Iowaville (1843–1870) occupies a hill west of

Selma on the north side of Highway 16 just before its intersection with
Acorn Avenue. The Iowaville cemetery marker commemorates historic figures like Black Hawk and James Jordan and events such as the westward
passage through here by members of the Church of Jesus Christ of Latter-
Day Saints (Mormons) in 1846. From the cemetery you can view the valley of
the Des Moines River and the general environs associated with all of these
events. An award-winning documentary series on the Ioway, *Lost Nation:
The Ioway*, by Kelly and Tammy Rundle of Fourth Wall Films, explores their
past and present history. See www.iowaymovie.com/.

✳ WANT TO LEARN MORE?

Foster, Lance M.

2000   Closing Circle: Musings on the Iowa Indians in Iowa. In *The
World Between Two Rivers: Perspectives on American Indians in Iowa*, ed.
Gretchen M. Bataille, David Mayer Gradwohl, and Charles I. P.
Silet, 142–150. Iowa City: University of Iowa Press.

Haury-Artz, Chérie

2013   *A River Runs through It: Life along the Des Moines River*. Office of the
State Archaeologist, University of Iowa, Iowa City.

Peterson, Cynthia L., ed.

2013   *Archaeological Study of Iowaville, a 1765–1824 Ioway (Báxoje) Village in Van
Buren County, Iowa*. Contract Completion Report 1956. Office of the
State Archaeologist, University of Iowa, Iowa City.

2014   Iowaville, a 1765–1820 Báxoje (Ioway) Village. *Journal of the Iowa
Archeological Society* 61.

Schwartz, Saul G.

2008   Iowaville: Ioway and the 18th-Century Fur Trade in Southeast Iowa.
Newsletter of the Iowa Archaeological Society 58(3): 4–5.

Wedel, Mildred M.

1981   The Ioway, Oto, and Omaha Indians in 1700. *Journal of the Iowa
Archeological Society* 28:1–13.

1986   Peering at the Ioway Indians through the Mist of Time: 1650–circa
1700. *Journal of the Iowa Archeological Society* 33:1–74.

28 Bonaparte Pottery: Industrial Archaeology in Iowa

✳ *Bonaparte, Van Buren County*

✳ *Historic*

✳ SITE NUMBER 13VB200

THE APPEARANCE OF early pottery factories in Iowa soon followed the opening of the territory in 1832. Early potteries produced redware, a ceramic material that resembles glazed terra-cotta, and stoneware, a hard, thick ceramic used in jugs and crocks. The ceramic industry often sprang up alongside Iowa coal mining. Ready access to river transport, local timber for fuel, and suitable clays, found in association with coal seams, presented the ideal ingredients for the manufacture of ceramic jars, jugs, crocks, and bowls for domestic food storage as well as drainage tiles, tubing, and chimney stacks for farms and towns. From rural, makeshift kilns, the pottery industry expanded throughout the 19th century, reaching a peak in the 1880s with centers at Fort Dodge, Des Moines, Sioux City, and Davenport.

The Bonaparte Pottery (originally the Parker-Hanbeck Pottery, 1866–1895) on the Des Moines River in Van Buren County lies at the heart of the largest concentration of historic potteries in Iowa. The 1876 factory building still stands virtually unchanged, and architectural and archaeological research has uncovered intact remains of two types of brick kilns, one circular and one linear, as well as a huge dump. This dump, called a waster midden or waster pit, contained thousands of sherds of discarded broken pottery, whole pots and molds, and blobs of ceramic called "kiln furniture," which were used to separate pots during firing.

Today, visitors to the site can tour the three-story factory building, view remnants of both kilns, and see a 6-feet-long cross section of the waster midden that once extended 150 feet along the Des Moines riverbank. Clay splatters on the walls and ceiling of the factory, the clay handprints of pottery workers, and a worn spot on a wooden floor where a potter operated a wheel or lathe connect the past to the present in a very personal way.

Excavating the linear kiln at the Bonaparte Pottery, facing north, 1994, Van Buren County.

Maria Schroeder excavating a kiln, 1994, at the Bonaparte Pottery, Van Buren County.

Efforts to understand and preserve the site by Marilyn and Donnie Thomas, the property owners, resulted in its listing on the National Register of Historic Places, and its creation as a heritage tourism destination. Reproductions of stoneware vessels, including a characteristic brown glazed jar, using the original molds recovered from the site, are available for purchase.

☀ TO VISIT

The Bonaparte Pottery is located at 411 1st Street, Bonaparte. The site is part of the Bonaparte Historic Riverfront District. To request information on visiting, call 319-592-3620.

☀ WANT TO LEARN MORE?

Haury-Artz, Chérie

2013   *A River Runs through It: Life along the Des Moines River.* Office of the State Archaeologist, University of Iowa, Iowa City.

Rogers, Leah D., Cynthia L. Peterson, Maria F. Schroeder, and Fred A. Finney

1995   *The Bonaparte Pottery Site (13VB200): A.K.A. the Parker-Hanback-Wilson Pottery: Archaeological and Historical Investigation.* Contract Completion Report 444. Office of the State Archaeologist, University of Iowa, Iowa City.

29 The Not-So-Empty North

* Rice Lake State Park, Winneshiek County
* Archaic–Late Prehistoric
* SITE NUMBER 13WNII

WHEN ARCHAEOLOGISTS began systematically recording archaeological sites, they noticed a peculiar gap in the north-central part of Iowa.
Virtually no sites were recorded in the upper portion of the Des Moines
Lobe, a thumb-shaped region of north-central Iowa that was once covered
by the last glacier in Iowa, more than 10,000 years ago. Settlers considered
the region inhospitable until thousands of small wetlands were drained.
Did Indians also find this region inhospitable?

In the late 1970s, archaeologist Stephen Lensink led a project to fill in
the gap in the archaeology of the region. He interviewed area artifact collectors, cataloged their collections, and recorded the sites from which they
came. His team surveyed dozens of fields. He concluded that north-central
Iowa contained just as many sites as the rest of the state. They just had not
been recorded because of the comparatively low number of residents in the
Des Moines Lobe and the absence of archaeological survey — sites cannot
be recorded if no one is around to find them.

Lensink counted the different point types found in his study and grouped
them by age. He examined the environmental and climatic data for the region. It appeared that while the utilization of prairie resources remained
stable throughout most of prehistory, the marshes saw maximum use following dry periods, as the rejuvenation of their resources depended upon
periodic drying and subsequent flooding. Cooler and wetter episodes, like
the Late Archaic, discouraged utilization.

The collection of Arlo Johnson, of rural Hancock County, proved particularly informative to Lensink's research, not just because it contained
hundreds of artifacts from the Des Moines Lobe but also because Johnson
had carefully documented the sites where items were found and recorded
the artifacts using the Smithsonian Institution's Trinomial system. His collection still represents one of the best documented from the Des Moines

Knife River flint preforms found by Arlo Johnson, Hancock County.

Lobe. Over 200 archaeological sites were accurately mapped and recorded as a result of his efforts.

To display and share his discoveries, in 1940 Johnson built the Timberlake Museum on his farm. It remained open to the public during the summer and for tours by hundreds of area schoolchildren until his death 60 years later. At that time, the museum and the collection were donated and moved to Heritage Park in nearby Forest City.

✳ TO VISIT

The Arlo Johnson collection is available for public viewing at the Timberlake Museum in Heritage Park on the south edge of Forest City, along U.S. Highway 69. Rice Lake State Park near Lake Mills is a good example of a northern Iowa lake with several prehistoric sites nearby, including site 13WN11, which Charles R. Keyes recorded in 1929 as the depressions of three lodges 40 feet in diameter surrounded by an embankment. This site was possibly a Late Prehistoric Oneota settlement, although the depressions and embankment are no longer visible. Take I-35 to exit 214, head west on Highway 105, follow the signs to Rice Lake.

✳ WANT TO LEARN MORE?

Lensink, Stephen C.

1984 A Quantitative Model of Central-Place Foraging among Prehistoric Hunter-Gatherers. Ph.D. diss., University of Iowa, Iowa City.

1991 Arlo Johnson Wins 1991 Award. *Newsletter of the Iowa Archeological Society* 41(2): 3–4.

2000 In Memory of Arlo Johnson. *Newsletter of the Iowa Archeological Society* 50(4): 7.

30 Enigmatic Alignments at the Folkert Mound Group

✳ *Hardin County*

✳ *Woodland*

✳ SITE NUMBER 13HA30

NATIVE AMERICANS WERE sky watchers; the oral histories of almost all Indian tribes include stories about constellations and stars, and explanations for the moon and sun. This is not surprising, since the sky was the calendar that told people when to plant crops, when to move to new camps, and how much time until winter came or left. We know that some archaeological sites in prehistoric Mexico were astronomically aligned; there, whole cities were oriented to celestial plans, but evidence of this phenomenon is rare in the central United States. At Cahokia, the Mississippian center near St. Louis occupied 900 years ago, there was a "woodhenge," a huge circle of large, upright wooden posts that researchers usually interpret as an observatory. Other than that, though, midwestern archaeoastronomy is a speculative endeavor, and attempts at divining meaning from the alignment of features such as mounds are met with skepticism; we just do not have enough information to draw any certain conclusions.

In Hardin County, a large collection of mounds overlooking the Iowa River contains a strange assemblage of earthworks that suggests Iowa Indians also marked the sky. There are far more linear mounds at this site than anywhere else in central Iowa, and there is a cruciform-shaped mound, the only known one in the state. This mound group, named Folkert, after a landowner, was first recorded in 1973 by John Hotopp. This late discovery is remarkable, as people recorded most of the major Iowa mound groups in the late 19th or early 20th century, and is a testament to this site's remoteness and inaccessibility.

Hotopp made an accurate outline map of the Folkert group when he discovered it. When planners were considering alternate routes for a nearby highway in the first decade of the new century, they ended up avoiding the mounds, but it became clear that a preservation plan was needed. In 2007,

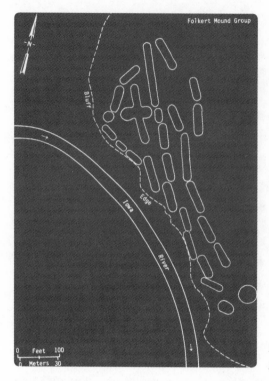

Map of the Folkert mound group, Hardin County.

archaeologists made a detailed topographic map of the mound group, and they also surveyed it with ground-penetrating radar. The radar did not detect much interior complexity within the mounds, but the detailed map revealed some curious alignments. If you draw lines connecting the knobs at the ends of the cruciform mound, called Mound X, and extend them south, the lines converge at Mound A, the largest mound at the site. Likewise, lines extended to the north from the knob ends of Mound X converge at the northern tip of the longest mound, Mound T.

Was this only a coincidence? George Horton, a respected amateur archaeologist and historian, suggested that at least one of the alignments corresponded to the location of the Crab Nebula supernova, which would have been quite prominent in the 11th century. However, Stephen Lensink, an archaeologist and amateur astronomer, ran digital historical astronomical reconstructions and concluded that none of the speculative alignments matched the location where the nebula would have risen or set in the 11th century.

William Whittaker
surveying the Folkert
mound group, Hardin
County.

Did the lines point to other ritual areas, such as different mound groups
or village sites or the cliffs at nearby Steamboat Rock? Archaeologist Chad
Goings calculated the site's viewshed, marking all the land that you can see
from the site. None of the extended alignments intercepted known mound
groups or prehistoric villages. While some alignments do point to Steamboat Rock, they are minor ones not involving Mound A or Mound X, and do
not point to any prominent landform or outcrop. At this time, it appears
the most likely explanation is that the alignments between Mound A and
Mound X are coincidental, and the people who built the remarkable Folkert
mound group were probably not using them as an observatory.

✳ TO VISIT

The land is in a remote area owned by the Hardin County Conservation
Board; there are plans to extend trails to the site in the future. Visit the
Calkins Nature Area and Interpretive Center, 18335 135th Street, Iowa Falls

(641-648-9878), for displays on area archaeology; it is open Monday–Sunday, mid-April–mid-October. Check the Conservation Board's web site for updates and information: www.hardincountyconservation.com.

✳ WANT TO LEARN MORE?

Collins, James, and William Whittaker
2007 Folkert Mound Group Revealed: Restoration and Non-Destructive Mapping of Hardin County Mounds. *Newsletter of the Iowa Archaeological Society* 57(1): 10.
2009 Alignments at the Folkert Mound Group. *Newsletter of the Iowa Archaeological Society* 59(1): 1–2.

Horton, George
2007 A Star Explodes! A.D. 1054: Did Prehistoric Native Iowans Witness and Record This Titanic Stellar Event? *Newsletter of the Iowa Archaeological Society* 57(3): 1–2.

Lensink, Stephen C.
2007 Notes on the Folkert Alignment. *Newsletter of the Iowa Archaeological Society* 57(3): 2.

31 Wanampito:
A Possible Ioway Site
from the 1600s

* Heery Woods State Park Nature Center, Clarksville, Butler County

* Late Prehistoric and Protohistoric

* SITE NUMBER 13BT16

LONG BEFORE INDIANS encountered Europeans, they owned European trade goods. Valuable objects, such as beads, medals, pots, and cloth, moved along traditional Indian trading networks, passing from village to village, hundreds of miles from where they were first obtained from European traders.

North of Waverly, about a mile from the Cedar River, is an unassuming cornfield that produced the best evidence in eastern Iowa for this dynamic period when European goods first arrived at Indian villages. Named Wanampito, Ioway for "blue bead," this site produced a stunning collection of Late Prehistoric artifacts, including triangular points, grinding stones, pottery, blue stone beads, and pipes, as well as European trade goods, including blue glass beads and a tinkler, a thin metal cone attached to clothing for decoration.

The Wanampito site is not near a major river, as one would expect, since trade goods often moved along rivers; its nearest surface water is an intermittent stream. It is possible that a spring once existed nearby, for the owner of the site reported that a perennial wet spot there had been drained. Collectors repeatedly visited the site to pick up large numbers of triangular Madison-style points. Fortunately, a collector donated his artifacts to the Heery Woods State Park Nature Center near Clarksville in the early 1990s.

Analysis of the glass beads by William Billeck, of the Smithsonian Institution, indicated they were manufactured in the 1600s. The earliest European maps of the site area date from the same period, and they show that the Ioway occupied the region. They lived near Spirit Lake in the 1680s and in southern Minnesota about 1700. By the 1740s, the Ioway had shifted to

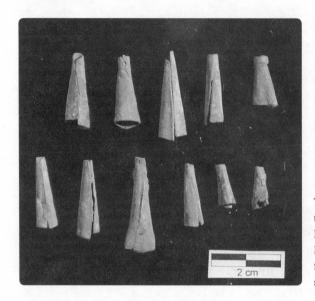

Tinkling cones similar to these from the Iowaville site, Van Buren County, were found at the Wanapito site, Butler County.

the south and west, living near the Missouri River. We think that the Wanampito site was the location of a small Ioway habitation.

Older Late Prehistoric sites, possibly also once residences of the Ioway, have been excavated near the Upper Iowa River (43) to the northeast. Slightly later in time, the French actually visited the Ioway at some of these locations. Contemporaneous or somewhat later Ioway sites much farther west, such as Gillett Grove and Blood Run (2), have also been excavated, as has Iowaville (27). Wanampito, however, is the only known site in the central part of the state that clearly bridges the gap from the Late Prehistoric to the early historic.

✳ TO VISIT

The Wanampito site is privately owned, and the landowners do not allow visits. Fortunately, a large collection of Wanampito artifacts, including dozens of points and a pipe carved from red catlinite stone, are on display at the Heery Woods State Park Nature Center just south of Clarksville. From Clarksville, drive south on Main Street, cross the Shell Rock River, and head west on 195th Street; follow the signs for the nature center.

✳ WANT TO LEARN MORE?

Whittaker, William E.

2010 Colin Betts on the Oneota, Protohistoric, and the Ioway. *Newsletter of the Iowa Archeological Society* 60(1): 8–9.

Whittaker, William E., and Mark L. Anderson

2008 Wanampito: An Early Ioway Site? *Newsletter of the Iowa Archeological Society* 58(1): 4–5.

32 Black Medicine Site, Hartman Reserve Nature Center: Conservation for the Sake of the Past

※ Blackhawk County
※ Woodland
※ SITE NUMBER 13BH164

JOHN HARTMAN, editor and general manager of the *Waterloo Daily Courier*, epitomizes Iowa's early citizen-archaeologists. Throughout his life, Hartman sustained an interest in the prehistory of Black Hawk County, which he shared in his newspaper. By the 1920s, when he began corresponding with Charles R. Keyes (see Weed Park Mounds [62]), he had been collecting artifacts and investigating sites — villages, camps, mounds, and even an Indian garden — for almost three decades. Artifacts from his collection still exist at the University of Northern Iowa (UNI). His conservation efforts also preserved many archaeological sites.

Inspired by Hartman's maps, notes, correspondence, and collection, UNI's Donald Gaff and students set out to relocate the Cedar Valley sites he had documented. On the same landform where Hartman recorded several mounds (many now gone), they discovered the Black Medicine site. The site rests atop a bluff overlooking a broad floodplain of the Cedar River in today's Hartman Reserve Nature Center. For four years, Gaff and his students investigated a multiperiod campsite repeatedly inhabited during the Middle Woodland through the Late Woodland periods. Madison-style arrow points and triangular side-notched points, along with three kinds of pottery — Linn Ware, Lane Farm, and Madison Ware — suggest successive occupations by late Middle Woodland, early Late Woodland, and terminal Woodland peoples.

The small-diameter post molds, remnants of former posts, that Gaff's students uncovered reflect the kind of light, temporary structures residents of Black Medicine constructed. A shallow hearth and lots of fire-cracked rock point to activities centered on cooking and roasting, perhaps meats, shell-fish, fish, tubers, or nuts. Then again, this evidence may have a "sweeter" interpretation. Could the ceramics and fire-cracked rock reflect collecting and boiling maple sap to make sugar? Although this activity is difficult to verify prehistorically, archaeologists predict that a maple sugar campsite might be expected to have few food remains, a relatively high ratio of pottery to chipped stone tools, hearths, and lots of fire-cracked rock, exactly the situation at Black Medicine. Gaff suggests the site's landscape position also meant maple trees were probably close by.

Temporary camps like Black Medicine did not exist in isolation but were part of a larger settlement pattern. Using Geographic Information Systems (GIS), Gaff and his students classified the Cedar Valley landscape into three types of resource zones—river, floodplain, and uplands. Then they considered the kinds of sites recorded in the region by Hartman and others (camps, stone tool workshops, villages, mounds) and mapped out their positions on the landscape. The results indicate that prehistoric peoples moved about strategically to take advantage of particular landscape settings and resources available within the three zones. Small groups probably revisited Black Medicine for days or weeks at a time to make use of specific short-term resources like maple sap or a variety of resources. Within

Lane Farm pottery, a style also found at the Black Medicine site, Black Hawk County.

a 15-to-60-minute walk from the site, the occupants could have reached resources in all three zones.

The prehistoric Waterloo area was a fairly complicated place at the end of the first millennium, with groups of people gathering in larger riverside camps or villages and then relocating as families or small work groups moved upriver seasonally to avail themselves of particular resources. Families and bands probably came together at special mound locations to bury and commemorate their dead.

John Hartman bequeathed not only useful archaeological information. His conservation efforts preserved some of the archaeological record itself. In 1938, he assisted the local YMCA in purchasing 56 acres of land for use as a camp and other community programs. In the 1970s, the Blackhawk County Conservation Board purchased additional property to create the 300-acre Hartman Reserve Nature Center, the largest undisturbed natural area in Black Hawk County.

✳ TO VISIT

The Black Medicine site, no longer visible above-ground, sits on a bluff top above the Cedar River in the Hartman Reserve Nature Center. The center is located at the Waterloo/Cedar Falls border, three blocks north of the intersection of Rainbow Drive and Laurie Avenue. From Highway 218, take the Greenhill Road exit and follow the signs. The interpretive center is open Monday–Friday and Sundays: www.hartmanreserve.org.

✳ WANT TO LEARN MORE?

Billeck, William T.
1987   Functional Variation at Two Short-Term, Multicomponent Sites in Black Hawk County, Iowa. *Journal of the Iowa Archeological Society* 34:7–22.

Gaff, Donald H., and Sarah J. Caldwell
2012   Traversing Field and Forest: John C. Hartman and Prehistoric Waterloo. *Journal of the Iowa Archeological Society* 59:1–12.

33 Was There a Walled Prehistoric Village along the Cedar Valley Nature Trail?

✳ *Black Hawk County*

✳ *Late Prehistoric*

✳ SITE NUMBER 13BH3

BLACK HAWK COUNTY has plenty of prehistoric sites, but seemingly very few mounds (see Black Medicine [32]). The county's largest river is the Cedar, and with a few exceptions, the Cedar River valley is enclosed by gradually sloping bluffs. It generally lacks the high imposing bluffs and terraces that mound builders seem to have preferred. Four miles east of La Porte City, the area where Spring Creek enters the Cedar River, was historically a rich landscape of wetlands, prairie, and forest that could have supported large villages. Indeed, there are prehistoric sites of the right time period for mounds, but the bluffs are so gradual that it is hard to imagine where the site occupants would have built them.

A nearby farmer with an interest in archaeology noticed artifacts in his field and, following his suspicions, surveyed the area for mounds in the 1960s. Near the juncture of Spring Creek and the Cedar River, he found three low embankments that may have been part of a prehistoric enclosure more than 400 feet across. To the south he noted several small mounds.

Archaeologist Darrell Fulmer recorded this site as 13BH3 in 1970, when he visited the farmer and made a map of the site. Fulmer did not excavate or collect any artifacts. Unfortunately, shortly after he visited the site, a dam transformed the area into a wetland lake. If the site could have been excavated or explored prior to this flooding, it might have been possible to determine if these embankments were part of a prehistoric village or if they were just odd landforms caused by old river meanders. If they were prehistoric, they would probably be Late Prehistoric, after A.D. 1300, and they would be one of the few examples from this part of the state. Perhaps the mounds and enclosed village, if it was a village, will emerge if

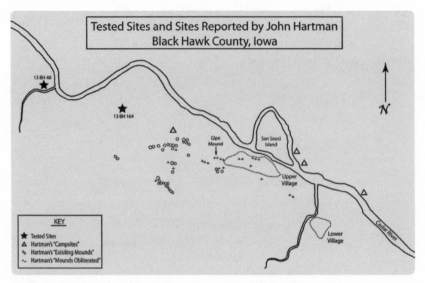

Map showing sites recorded by John Hartman, Blackhawk County. Courtesy of Donald Gaff.

the waters recede in the future. Early 20th-century newspaperman John Hartman also reported on village sites and mounds in the Cedar valley in Blackhawk County (see Black Medicine [32]).

✳ TO VISIT

The site is about 4 miles east of La Porte City. Bike, walk, or ski east along the Cedar Valley Nature Trail. Go past McFarlane Park, cross the Cedar River, and in about 1 mile you will cross Spring Creek on a long bridge. Soon there will be a small lake on the north side of the trail. This is where the possible mounds and enclosure stood.

✳ WANT TO LEARN MORE?

Morgan, Bob
2006 *Biking Iowa: 50 Great Road Trips and Trail Rides*. Madison, WI:
      Big Earth Publishing.

34 Wickiup Hill: Public Understanding and Preservation

* Linn County
* Archaic–Historic
* SITE NUMBER 13LN85

BETWEEN 1955 AND 1991, each one of Iowa's 99 counties created a county conservation program. Originating within the activism of conservationists such as Aldo Leopold and J. N. "Ding" Darling, such programs were meant to provide local outdoor recreational opportunities while promoting appreciation and preservation of natural resources. Today, Iowa county conservation boards (CCBs) continue to acquire, manage, and maintain thousands of acres of public lands and facilities that include natural areas, parks, campsites, trails, interpretive and recreation centers, and wildlife areas. Many of these properties contain important archaeological sites.

Wickiup Hill Outdoor Learning Center, situated along the left bank of the Cedar River in western Linn County and managed by the Linn County Conservation Department, stands out as a model in the documentation, interpretation, and preservation of the natural and cultural resources found within its 790 acres. Public events and state-of-the-art exhibits hosted at its interpretive center, signage along trails, and self-guided tours tell visitors about the people who formerly made the area home and utilized its diverse natural resources.

Beginning in 1994, archaeologists conducted a series of surveys and test excavations at Wickiup Hill to document the property's archaeological sites. The public assisted these endeavors via volunteer field schools, teacher workshops, and student archaeology camps. The results gave the Linn CCB information to protect and manage Wickiup Hill's archaeological sites and develop authentic educational programming.

Archaeologists recorded more than 20 sites within the river terraces, sand dunes, steep bluffs, and ridgetops that make up Wickiup Hill's landscape.

Wickiup Hill Outdoor Learning Center, Linn County. Photo by Jessica Rilling. Courtesy of Linn County Conservation Board.

Many represent multiperiod occupations, with prehistoric and historic oc-cupations stacked atop one another. They range from small, 5,000-year-old Archaic campsites, to clusters of Woodland mounds, to late 19th-century pioneer cabins. Woodland and historic sites are most common.

A particularly intriguing site is 13LN606, occupying a flat, woodland bench 46 feet above the Cedar River floodplain. Limited test excavations re-vealed both prehistoric and historic artifacts. The mid- to late 19th-century artifacts included glass items, including a blue glass bead, metal, buttons, ceramics, and three Indian head pennies, two minted in 1865 and the third in 1868. In one area of the site, archaeologists encountered an intact layer of flat, charred wooden boards, possibly remnants of a burned cabin floor. Nearby, and more enigmatic, was an oval basin, 20 inches deep, containing a ring of dolomite slabs and other rock, the interior filled with flecks of charcoal and burned earth. While this could represent a historic alcohol still, it might be a Native American sweat lodge.

The Wickiup Hill property is part of the traditional territory occupied by the Meskwaki in the early to mid-19th century before they ceded their Iowa lands. Early accounts also identify the Ho-Chunk (Winnebago) living here before the 1830s. American settlers reported a major winter camp of 300 Meskwaki, called "Wickiup Hollow," within the boundaries of present-day Wickiup Hill. Although forced from the state in 1846, many Meskwaki soon returned in secret. Others never left. Numerous references document Meskwaki encounters with Euroamerican settlers in Linn County, including along the Cedar River, throughout most of the 19th century. Here, they continued to hunt and camp in familiar areas, and it is likely that historic American Indian sites at Wickiup Hill, perhaps 13LN606 itself, testify to this presence. In 1856, with the permission of the state legislature, many Meskwaki returned to occupy land they purchased along the Iowa River in Tama County.

✳ TO VISIT

Wickiup Hill Outdoor Learning Center is located at 10260 Morris Hills Road, Toddville, in western Linn County, about 9 miles from downtown Cedar Rapids. From I-380, take the Boysen Road exit (25) west. Follow signage. Open Monday–Friday 8 a.m.–4:30 p.m.; Saturday 10 a.m.–4 p.m.; and Sunday 1 p.m.–4 p.m. Exhibits focus on the Meskwaki and earlier Ioway residents. Walking trails with interpretive signage pass some archaeological sites.

The Meskwaki Cultural Center and Museum, 349 Meskwaki Road, west of Tama, has displays of Meskwaki history and culture, and is open weekdays (641-484-3185).

✳ WANT TO LEARN MORE?

Green, William, comp. and ed.
1998 *Field Trip Guide: Wickiup Hill Outdoor Learning Center, Linn County, Iowa.* Office of the State Archaeologist, University of Iowa, Iowa City.

Rogers, Leah D.
1998 Accompanying Papers: Wickiup Hill Regional Historical Contexts. In *Field Trip Guide: Wickiup Hill Outdoor Learning Center, Linn County, Iowa,* comp. and ed. William Green, 33–42. Office of the State Archaeologist, University of Iowa, Iowa City.

1999   Wickiup Hill Iowa Archeological Society Fieldschool. *Newsletter of the Iowa Archeological Society* 49(3): 5, 7.

Rogers, Leah D., and William Green
1995   *Wickiup Hill Natural Area Archaeological Survey.* Research Papers 20, no. 3. Office of the State Archaeologist, University of Iowa, Iowa City.

CM

Catlinite tablet found
at the Blood Run site,
Lyon County (scanned
and highlighted by
Carol Moxham, Midwest
Archaeological Center,
and Angela Collins, Office
of the State Archaeologist).
Courtesy of Dale R. Hen-
ning and the University
of Iowa Office of the State
Archaeologist.

Blood Run National Historic Landmark, Lyon County.
Photo by John Pearson, Iowa Department of Natural Resources.

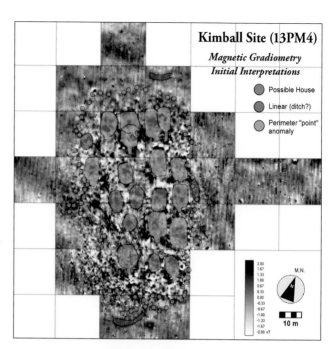

Results of geophysical survey at the Kimball Village site, showing suspected location of houses, palisade, and ditch, Plymouth County. Map created by Archaeo-Imaging Lab, University of Arkansas, Fayetteville.

Kimball Site (13PM4)

Magnetic Gradiometry
Initial Interpretations

- Possible House
- Linear (ditch?)
- Perimeter "point" anomaly

2.00
1.67
1.33
1.00
0.67
0.33
0.00
-0.33
-0.67
-1.00
-1.33
-1.67
-2.00 nT

M.N.

10 m

Projectile points (probably arrow points) from the Kimball Village site, Plymouth County.

Incised and cut bone artifact from the Kimball Village site, Plymouth County.

Artifact sampler, Late Prehistoric sites, western Iowa.

Artist's drawing of the Wittrock Indian Village site, O'Brien County.

Projectile points (spear or dart points) from the Cherokee Sewer site, Cherokee County.

Oneota ceramic vessel, Dixon site, Woodbury County.

Kevin Verhulst, Office of the State Archaeologist, working at the Davis-Oriole site, 2008, Mills County.

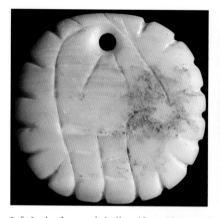
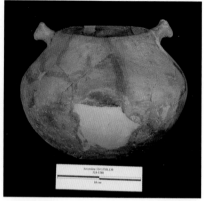

Left: Incised mussel shell artifact, Glenwood culture site 13ML39, Mills County.
Right: Glenwood culture "Bean Pot," Glenwood culture site 13ML130, Mills County.

Distribution of
known Glenwood
culture houses
in Iowa showing
proximity to the
mouth of the Platte
River.

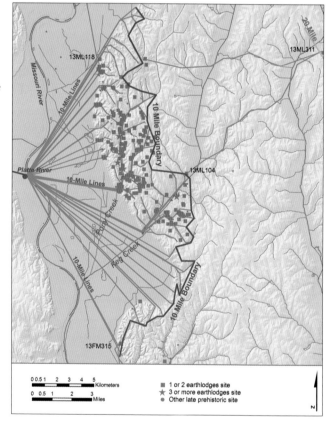

Governor's mansion, Terrace Hill, Des Moines, Polk County.

Modern garden scene, Terrace Hill, Des Moines, Polk County.

Beaux Arts fountain, unearthed on the east side of the World Food Prize Building, formerly the city library, Des Moines, Polk County.

Excavation at the Palace site, 2010, Des Moines, Polk County.

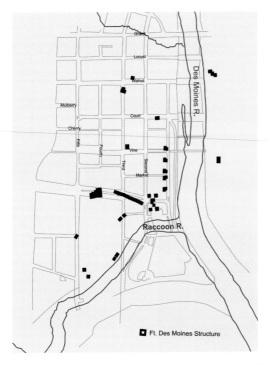

Map showing building and
other features unearthed
at Fort Des Moines 2,
Polk County.

Map showing the location of
prehistoric and historic sites
uncovered in downtown
Des Moines, Polk County.

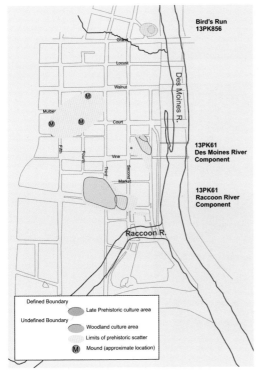

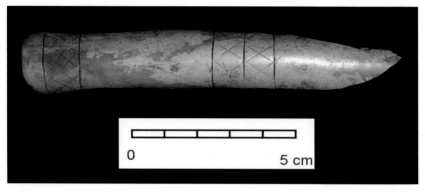

Polished and incised bone artifact, Iowaville site, Van Buren County.

Pottery sherd recovered from the Iowaville site, Van Buren County.

Fine-screened sample showing colored glass trade beads, bone fragments, and stone tool flakes and fire-cracked rock recovered from the Iowaville site, Van Buren County.

Metal gun barrels recovered from the Iowaville site, Van Buren County.

Volunteer Earl Walrath assisting resistivity survey at the Iowaville site, Van Buren County.

Ceramic jug and faceted jar from the Bonaparte Pottery, Van Buren County.

Waster midden, Bonaparte Pottery, Van Buren County.

Myre Slough, Winnebago County.

Above: Catlinite elbow pipe, Wanampito site, Heery Woods State Park Nature Center, Butler County.

Right: Late Woodland Madison-style projectile point (probably arrow point). Courtesy Christian Driver.

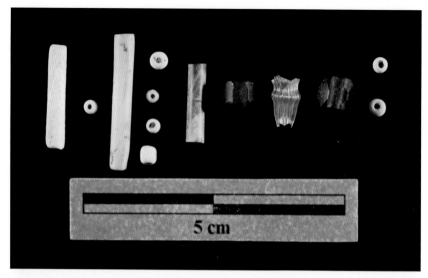

Shell and glass beads, Patterson Trading Post site, Iowa County.

Artifacts from the Patterson Trading Post site, Iowa County.

Left: Volunteer Joanne Peterson, screening soil from the Patterson Trading Post site, 2012, Iowa County.

Right: Coin from the Patterson Trading Post site, Iowa County.

Amana fish weir, 2012, composite photo showing Iowa River and estimated location of weir marked in yellow. Facing west-southwest.

Woodpecker Cave field school excavations, 2013, by the University of Iowa, Department of Anthropology, Iowa City, Johnson County.

Plum Grove field school excavations, facing northwest, 1997, by the University of Iowa, Department of Anthropology, Iowa City, Johnson County.

Effigy Mounds National Monument, Allamakee and Clayton Counties.

Effigy Mounds National Monument, Allamakee and Clayton Counties.

William Whittaker conducting a ground-penetrating-radar survey at the Sny Magill mound group, Clayton County.

Officers' barracks, now the fort museum, facing northwest, Fort Atkinson State Preserve, Winneshiek County.

Above: Reconstructing the picket stockade at Fort Atkinson State Preserve, 2006, Winneshiek County.

Right: Quarry, source of building stone at Fort Atkinson State Preserve, Winneshiek County. Photo by John Pearson, Iowa Department of Natural Resources.

Julien Dubuque's monument, Mines of Spain, Dubuque County.

Maquoketa Caves State Park, Jackson County.

Right: Removing charred residue on pottery rim from Mouse Hollow rockshelter, Jackson County.

Below: Mississippian Ramey-style pottery rim, Mouse Hollow rockshelter, Jackson County.

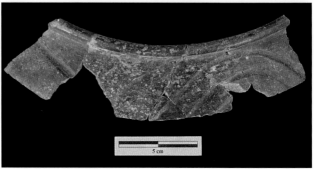

5 cm

Hurstville Lime Kiln, Jackson County.

Antoine Le Clair House, Davenport, Scott County.

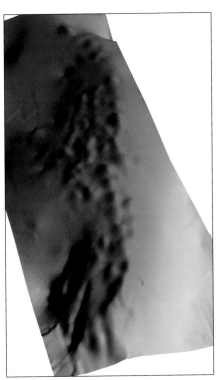

Shaded relief map showing mounds at Malchow Mounds, Louisa County.

Living history at reconstructed Fort Madison, Lee County, Iowa.

35 Patterson Trading Post

☀ *Iowa County*

☀ *Historic*

☀ SITE NUMBER 13IW261

THE FIRST HALF OF the 19th century witnessed the rapid cession of Iowa's Indian lands to the U.S. government, and, after 1838, legally to Euroamerican settlers. Between 1815 and 1842, the Meskwaki (and Sauk) signed successive treaties forcing the sale of their eastern Iowa lands and the relocation of their villages. Traders quickly sought out these new settlements and set up trading houses or posts nearby. The pattern of posts established at a dozen eastern Iowa locations mirrors the tribes' own westward exodus as they ceded their lands. If archaeologists can pin down the location of one of the post sites, they may be able to find the nearby village site as well. Such was the case with the Patterson Trading Post site and the nearby Meskwaki village.

In the spring of 1839, the Meskwaki leader Wacoshashe and his band occupied a village along the Iowa River near modern-day South Amana. The following year Meskwaki Chief Poweshiek and his band joined them. Other Meskwaki soon followed. Just as quickly, the Western Department of the American Fur Company, managed by Pierre Chouteau and Company of St. Louis, established a trading house adjacent to Wacochache's village. Their agents, the Phelps brothers, supervised the post, which was apparently managed by a trader named Nathaniel Patterson.

Trading records, ledgers, maps, newspaper articles, and early correspondence hinted at the location of the Patterson Trading Post site. Most revealing was the General Land Office (GLO) survey map of 1843, which illustrated a cabin labeled "Trading House." A slightly later account described the "old double log cabin that then constituted the trading house." Early documents also referenced a Meskwaki cemetery and campsite in the same vicinity.

Generally, frontier trading posts were little more than cabins, sometimes with cellars, a number of smaller outbuildings for storage, and occasionally a stockade. The trader stocked personal items for himself and perhaps

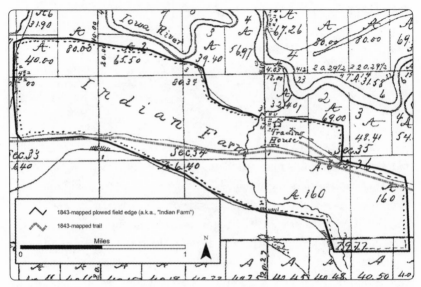

1843 Government Land Office survey map showing location of the Patterson "Trading House," Iowa County.

his family, as well as goods shipped to him from the trading company for barter to the Indian suppliers. Commodities purchased from Native Americans, such as meat, beeswax, tallow, honey, and maple sugar, were key to his personal survival.

Archaeologist Cynthia Peterson, from the OSA, with the support of the Amana Heritage Society and the Amana Colonies Land Use District, explored the area of the suspected post as noted on the GLO map. A helpful South Amana resident provided additional clues, suggesting that this was the right spot. Her collection of artifacts from the surface of what is a modern farm field today included thimbles, glass beads, and gunflints—the exact kinds of items traded during the period.

The archaeologists, with an enthusiastic volunteer crew, surveyed the site with a metal detector and excavated auger holes and test squares. The excavations uncovered buried features including a deep pit and a trash-filled cellar, both containing dozens of artifacts. Glass beads, a lead bale seal used to secure and identify parcels of fur and cloth, and small pieces of silver and worked copper were clearly Meskwaki trade items. Other artifacts duplicated items listed on trade inventories: gun parts, smoking

Volunteers excavating at the Patterson Trading Post site, 2012, Iowa County.

pipes, horse tack, mirrors, harmonicas, mouth harp, iron axes, knives, bone buttons, fasteners, needles, pins, glassware, and dishes. In addition, the Meskwaki would have received commodities such as cloth (a favored item), ribbon, gunpowder, food, and horses. The discovery of an 1838 half-dime supported the 1839–1843 post occupation date. There is little doubt that the remnants of the Patterson trading post had been found.

The fieldwork at the trading post site also provided an opportunity to hunt for the suspected Meskwaki village. The recollections of an early Amana resident described a former Indian village east of the trading post site. A careful surface survey of this area quickly revealed the presence of 1830s–1840s period artifacts. Glass beads, gunflints, horse tack, lead bars, a bear ankle bone with metal knife cut marks, an entire clay pipe bowl, and many smoking pipe fragments intermingled with kitchen items, including fragments of glass, crockery, and earthenware—almost certainly remnants of the village.

Beginning in 1825, the federal government allowed traders to deduct Indian debts from the annuity payments tribes received as part of treaty agreements. In the case of the Meskwaki, and the Sauk, high trading debt forced their final land cession in 1842. With this final cession the Meskwaki left their village and moved west yet again, with most of the tribe ultimately leaving Iowa altogether by 1846. Following their departure, the Patterson trading post became a residence and general store. In 1855, the Community of True Inspiration (Amana Society) purchased the property and the surrounding fields.

Future research at the Patterson Trading Post site and nearby Meskwaki village site promises to contribute information crucial to our understanding of the frontier fur trade and Indian removal in Iowa.

✳ TO VISIT

The Patterson Trading Post and nearby Meskwaki village sites are on private land owned by the Amana Society, Inc., which does not permit access. Follow 220th Trail north from South Amana across the Iowa River to experience the environs of these sites. The area is also encompassed within the Iowa Valley Scenic Byway. The byway loop that encompasses the historic Amana Colonies, including South Amana, is within close proximity to the Patterson Trading Post and Meskwaki village sites: www.iowabyways.org /iowa-valley. The Meskwaki Cultural Center and Museum, 349 Meskwaki Road, west of Tama, has displays of Meskwaki history and culture, and is open weekdays (641-484-3185).

✳ WANT TO LEARN MORE?

Peterson, Cynthia L.

2012 *Three Meskwaki-Related Sites near South Amana, Iowa: The Patterson Trading Post (13IW261), the Village of Wacoshashe and Poweshiek (13IW258), and a Mortuary Site (13IW257)*. Contract Completion Report 1915. Office of the State Archaeologist, University of Iowa, Iowa City.

36 Easy Fishing on the Iowa River

※ *Iowa County*

※ *Late Prehistoric or Historic*

※ SITE NUMBER 13IW100

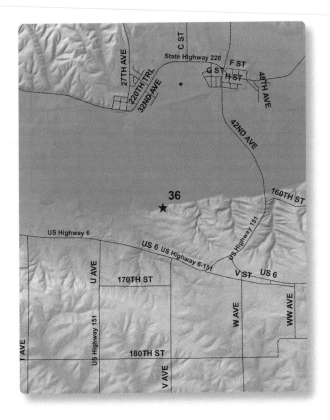

IN 1844, government surveyors noticed something very odd—a rock dam across the Iowa River more than 1 mile from the nearest trail, more than 5 miles from the nearest Indian village, and more than 20 miles from the nearest American settlement, Iowa City. Why was there a dam in the middle of nowhere?

It was a Native American fish weir, a V-shaped low dam that funneled fish to a narrow spot in the river, where they could be easily netted. The weir soon became a local landmark as the Amana Colonies grew around

Amana fish weir, 1976, Iowa County.

it; schoolchildren took field trips to visit it, and romantics often made the easy hike to explore it. It remained an excellent location to catch fish well into the 20th century, but it became harder to find when dams were built downriver and water levels rose.

The age of the weir is unknown, but a reasonable speculation is that it was built in the very early historic period by the Meskwaki, who had a village to the west. Fish weirs require a lot of rock, and this was the spot on the river closest to the Meskwaki village where the Iowa ran along bedrock. Elsewhere, the river flows through rock-free silt. The river historically meandered quite a bit and did not stay in a channel for long before creating a new one, which suggests the weir was not that old in 1844.

The river keeps shifting, even today. The drought of 1988–1989 seems to be the last time anyone saw the V-shaped portion of the weir. The flood of 1993 probably accelerated a shift in the river. By 1999, the Iowa River had drifted north of the weir's V, and only a portion of rip-rap extending from the north end of the weir could be seen. After 1999, a series of wet years made even this portion invisible. A comparison of aerial photos from the 2000s shows the Iowa River steadily drifting north, and the weir became absorbed in the south bank. A visit to the site during the drought of 2012 revealed that the weir was no longer visible, and was probably buried beneath 5 feet of silt a great distance south of the current river channel.

The disappearance of the weir is not all bad news. While it deprives Iowans of a scenic reminder of Native Americans' abilities and ingenuity, the burial of the weir in silt likely preserved it for the future. We have a very good idea about the weir's location, and it is now deeply buried and protected for future research.

✳ TO VISIT

The fish weir site is a pleasant hike of a few hours when visiting the Amana Colonies. From Amana take U.S. 151 south, or from Iowa City take U.S. 6 west to the intersection of U.S. 151 and U.S. 6. The trailhead is well marked, with parking and a picnic area. Along the trail is a fine group of conical mounds, marked on the trail signs, and the view at the end of the trail overlooking the weir site is very scenic. At the bluff, look west along the river; the weir is buried in the scrubby grass south of the river, closer to the south bluffs. Someday the river may shift and expose the weir again. The Meskwaki Cultural Center and Museum, 349 Meskwaki Road, west of Tama, has displays of Meskwaki history and culture, and is open weekdays (641-484-3185). The Amana Heritage Museum, 4310 220th Trail, Amana, is open April–October, and sometimes has exhibits on the Meskwaki: www.amanaheritage.org/museums.html.

✳ WANT TO LEARN MORE?

Jones, Douglas W.

2003 A Fishy Story from Iowa Some Preliminary Considerations of Prehistoric Fishing Practices on the Eastern Prairie-Plains. *Journal of the Iowa Archeological Society* 50 85–98.

Whittaker, John C.

1989 Experimental Fishing at the Amana Fish Weir. *Newsletter of the Iowa Archeological Society* 39(1): 1–2.

Whittaker, William E.

2013 The Disappearance of the Amana Indian Fish Weir. *Newsletter of the Iowa Archeological Society* 63(1): 1–5.

37 Excavating the Excavations at Ginger Stairs

☀ *Palisades-Kepler State Park, Linn County*

☀ *Archaic and Woodland*

☀ SITE NUMBER 13LN215

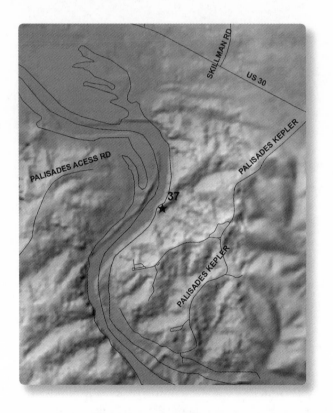

ON JUNE 17, 1930, Charles R. Keyes brought a class of summer school students from Cornell College to what is now Palisades-Kepler State Park southwest of Mount Vernon; their goal was to find and excavate a rockshelter. Rockshelters are overhangs of rock in a cliff face that Native Americans often camped beneath, attracted by the protection they provide from rain, snow, and sun. Rockshelters often have excellent artifact preservation because they can trap airborne soil, also called loess, which can bury the floor quickly, and the rock overhang keeps out rainwater, creating a stable environment that aids preservation.

Although the imposing cliffs lining the Cedar River gave the Palisades its name, the park does not have many large rockshelters. Luckily, Keyes's class found a promising, if small, shelter in what is now the north end of the park. It was one of the few rockshelters with a level floor large enough for a small group to sleep in. It was difficult to get to, accessible only by a small steep trail. Students had to walk gingerly, so perhaps that's why the site was nicknamed Ginger Stairs, or perhaps because wild ginger is common in Palisades-Kepler State Park. Keyes wrote in his notes that he planned to change the name, but it stuck.

That summer his students excavated much of the level talus slope in front of the shelter; a talus is a band of rock and soil that develops below a cliff, made of fallen rocks and loess trapped by the cliff. The trench was 18 feet long and about 5 feet wide and 3 feet deep; the soil containing artifacts was about 2 feet deep. Keyes made very limited notes, including a sketch map and some passing comments on the artifacts found: "three flint points, many mussel shells, a few animal bones, a few fragments of turtle carapace, a few flint chips, many potsherds, many fire-place stones of limestone, burned red" was a typical entry.

Fifteen years later, Keyes returned to Ginger Stairs. It is not clear from his notes where he excavated in 1945, but the notes, together with the artifacts he found, indicate it was the interior of the shelter. The location and extent of the excavation are unknown, but he later commented that he investigated most of it. He found far fewer artifacts within the shelter than outside it, and he encountered no evidence of the spectacular organic preservation that often exists at other shelters. About this time he also dug a few small holes at a nearby smaller shelter, which he called Ginger Stairs II. From Ginger Stairs II, he kept only one large ground stone.

Keyes never formally wrote up or published his excavation results; his notes on these sites were mixed in with innumerable notes of other excavations and discoveries, and the artifacts eventually made their way to the OSA and to museums. While writing his 1959 dissertation, Wilfred Logan reexamined the Ginger Stairs material. For unknown reasons, he changed the site name to "Gingerstairs."

James Zalesky standing in front of the Ginger Stairs I Rockshelter, view from the southwest, 1980, Linn County.

Logan's reanalysis, finally published in 1976, was hampered by a mistake made by an earlier lab technician. One of the artifact boxes from Ginger Stairs I that contained the 1930s items from the exterior excavation was inexplicably labeled Ginger Stairs II on paper tags in the box. It is clearly not from Ginger Stairs II, since the grinding stone from Ginger Stairs II is in a separate box labeled as such, and the artifacts in the mislabeled box match those Keyes described finding in the exterior excavation of Ginger Stairs I. Because of this mislabeling, Logan erroneously thought he was dealing with two sites, Gingerstairs I, which was actually the interior of the Ginger Stairs I shelter, and Gingerstairs II, which was actually the 1930s excavation of the talus of Ginger Stairs I.

To make sense of the Ginger Stairs excavations, we have to "excavate" the work of two archaeologists: Keyes, who took poor notes but left a few clues, and Logan, who performed a commendable analysis but was misled by faulty artifact labeling. Reading from Keyes's notes, the Ginger Stairs talus excavation of 1930 contained the vast majority of artifacts, including all points and most pottery that could be associated with a particular time period. The talus slope did not appear to be stratified; Keyes found heated rock at all levels, but no distinct hearths. Pottery appears to have been found

Late Woodland Minott's Ware pottery similar to this from the Mouse Hollow rockshelter in Jackson County was found at the Ginger Stairs I Rockshelter, Linn County.

Artifacts excavated by Charles R. Keyes, Ginger Stairs I Rockshelter, Linn County.

at all levels, as were points of different ages, but this is difficult to know for sure, since none of the artifacts are coded by level or depth. The pottery was largely Late Woodland styles called Madison Ware and Minott's Ware. Points indicated that people had used the site periodically throughout prehistory, with a mix of Early Archaic, Early Woodland, and Late Woodland points. The interior of the shelter was excavated in two levels, 0–12 inches and 12–30 inches, and contained few artifacts, but Keyes did recover a nice Late Woodland clay pipe. There was no obvious stratification in the shelter deposits.

The Ginger Stairs rockshelter excavation represents a transitional period in Iowa archaeology. Earlier excavators would only have searched for interesting objects and kept few notes or bone or flakes. Ideas like provenience and context were becoming important, but a lot of the concepts and methods used in modern archaeology, including digging in levels, square units, identifying soil strata, soil screening, and detailed note taking, were not commonly utilized. Because Keyes took and kept notes and saved most of the artifacts he found, it is possible to make sense of what was found at Ginger Stairs.

✴ TO VISIT

Palisades-Kepler State Park is southwest of Mount Vernon, and southeast of Cedar Rapids, on the south side of U.S. Highway 30, about 4 miles west of State Highway 1. Keep right as you enter the park; enjoy the prehistoric Woodland mounds that run alongside the main park road. Park in any lot near the trail system. Follow the main river foot trail at Palisades-Kepler north to the north end of the park. Find one of the smaller foot trails that leads to the river; Ginger Stairs I and II are along the river, up the steep talus slope, so you'll have to walk gingerly.

✴ WANT TO LEARN MORE?

Logan, Wilfred D.

1976 *Woodland Complexes in Northeastern Iowa.* Publications in Archeology 15. National Park Service, U.S. Department of the Interior, Washington D.C.

38 Woodpecker Cave

✳ *Johnson County*

✳ *Archaic–Historic*

✳ SITE NUMBER 13JH202

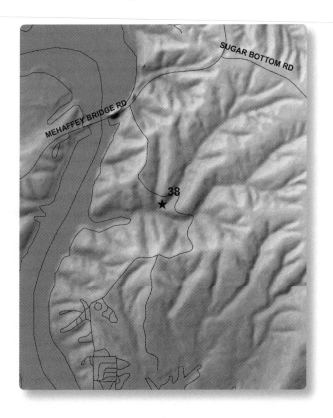

FOR MILLENNIA, people found natural shelter beneath the eroded cliffs of eastern Iowa's Devonian-age limestone and dolomites. "Woodpecker Cave," or "Indian Cave," is a shallow rockshelter perched above a small tributary stream of the Iowa River. The cavern opens to the south and east, offering a warm, sunny exposure in the winter and blocking the prevailing winds.

Large public works programs, especially the construction of dams and reservoirs, threatened archaeological sites in the mid-20th century. In order to salvage information from the doomed sites, an "army" of archaeologists,

Warren W. Caldwell's 1956 excavation of the Woodpecker Cave site, Johnson County, for the Smithsonian Institution's Bureau of American Ethnology.

under the auspices of the Smithsonian Institution's River Basin Surveys (RBS) program, recorded and excavated hundreds of sites.

In 1938, the U.S. Army Corps of Engineers acquired over 32,700 acres of land along the Iowa River to create the Coralville Dam and Reservoir. By the time the project was completed 20 years later, archaeological research had documented dozens of new sites, including mounds, campsites, and habitations, several of which were excavated. A highlight was Woodpecker Cave. Its deep, abundant, and well-preserved deposits offered a glimpse of the lives of people who occupied the shelter for thousands of years.

The residents of Woodpecker Cave were confined to an irregular living space about 350 square feet, protected beneath the shelter's rock overhang. They dug shallow hearths, and detritus from cooking, eating, and stone-tool making was tossed out over the talus slope in front of the shelter (see Ginger Stairs [37]). Some bits, however, were tromped into the shelter's dirt floor. Later, animals burrowed into the deposits, creating holes and dirt piles. Earthworms nosed dirt up and down. Soil blew in, and rock and sand fell from the ceiling to the floor. Each subsequent group of human residents created their own layer of "life." Over time, the deposits grew, and the floor of the shelter came closer to the ceiling.

The RBS's Warren Caldwell and his 11-member crew dug almost all of the 8.5-feet-deep rockshelter, stopping when they encountered bedrock. Their research defined two major layers. The topmost contained a rich but apparently mixed assortment of stone tools, pottery, discarded animal bones, and mussel shells from different times and cultures. In the ashy soils of the lower layer, they found a less-revealing array of discarded bone and stone flakes. Diagnostic artifacts, pottery, and stone projectile points confirmed that people used the shelter intermittently and probably seasonally for more than 3,000 years. They ate mussels in abundance, as well as deer, woodchucks, raccoons, dogs, gophers, cottontail rabbits, walnuts, hickory nuts, and hazelnuts.

The most intensive period of activity seems to have been during the Late Woodland period about a millennium ago. While the Late Woodland pottery found was typical of that at similar period sites in eastern Iowa, a small amount came from western Iowa's Great Oasis culture sites like Cowan (4). Its presence in Woodpecker Cave shows that communities living hundreds of miles from one another were in contact 1,000 years ago.

More recent and precise research at Woodpecker Cave, including digital photography and three-dimensional mapping by the University of Iowa, has demonstrated a more complicated picture of well-preserved and intact deposits still existing within the shelter and the talus slope that fronts it. This bodes well for expanding the story of the site's earliest inhabitants.

✳ TO VISIT

From I-380, take exit 4 to North Liberty, turn east onto Penn Street, follow to N Front Street (aka Mehaffey Bridge Road), turn north. After crossing Mehaffey Bridge, turn south and follow the entrance road. Park a vehicle in the turnout above the Cedar Valley Nature Trail. Follow the trail to the south.

✳ WANT TO LEARN MORE?

Artz, Joe Alan, and Lynn M. Alex

2009   Flood Effects on Archaeological Sites. In *A Watershed Year: Anatomy of the Iowa Floods of 2008*, ed. Cornelia F. Mutel, 123–129. Iowa City: University of Iowa Press.

Caldwell, Warren

1961   *Archaeological Investigations at the Coralville Reservoir.* Bureau of American Ethnology, Bulletin 179, River Basin Surveys Papers No. 22, 79–148. Washington, D.C.

Enloe, James G., and Theodore Marks

2013   Excavations at Woodpecker Cave — University of Iowa Archaeological Field School 2012. Report on file, Department of Anthropology, University of Iowa, Iowa City.

Morrow, Toby A.

1997   Previous Archaeological Work in Johnson County, Iowa. In *Archaeology and History of Indian and Pioneer Settlement*, ed. Cynthia L. Peterson, 97–101. Contract Completion Report 492. Office of the State Archaeologist, University of Iowa, Iowa City.

Overstreet, David F.

1985   The Archaeology of Coralville Lake, Iowa, Vol. 5: Site Specific Data Base. *Reports of Investigation 167.* Great Lakes Archaeological Research Center, Wauwatosa, WI.

39 Edgewater Park Site

* Coralville, Johnson County
* Archaic
* SITE NUMBER 13JHI132

THE EARLIEST European explorers described Native Americans as excellent farmers, living in large villages surrounded by gardens and crop fields. Indians, however, were not always farmers; for most of prehistory, they ate only wild plants and animals. The change to agriculture was gradual and took about 3,000 years in North America. Hunting and gathering wild foods became less important, and raising plants became more important. Archaeologically, plants appeared in new areas, and plants changed in appearance as they were bred to be more productive.

The Edgewater Park site in Coralville had evidence of the earliest stages of this change. Archaeologists from the OSA discovered the site while surveying the area that is now the Iowa River Landing in Coralville prior to its development. The site was found about 4 feet below surface. Excavation proved very slow, since the site rested below the water table and had to be continuously pumped. Archaeologists used this water to wash excavated soil through fine mesh, which resulted in the collection of very small artifacts. Although little could be seen in the muddy clay during excavation, the residue of burned earth and charcoal, small stone flakes, and butchered animal bone made it possible to determine the location of hearths, flint-knapping (stone-tool making) areas, and butchering spots. Soil samples from the site contained seeds of little barley, a plant that is not native to the area, and barnyard grass, a local plant similar to millet. Both of these plants would later be domesticated.

The people at the Edgewater Park site 3,800 years ago were mobile hunters and gatherers. Their site was a temporary camp along the Iowa River where the inhabitants chipped stone tools, including hunting weapons; sat around at least two hearths; and fished and hunted. The types of stone used for tools suggested they had just come downriver from central or northern Iowa, and plants found at the site indicated camping in late summer or early fall. It is reasonable to assume that they were probably heading south,

Excavations at the Edgewater Park site, 2006, Iowa River in background,
Johnson County.

and the site offered a good spot to rest and resupply before continuing their
trip toward the Mississippi River valley for winter.

Other people were beginning to grow domesticated plants in the southern Mississippi River region at this time, and it is likely that the people at
the Edgewater Park site were directly or indirectly in contact with them.
While the occupants did not grow crops, they were changing the way they
produced food, shifting toward plants that would later be domesticated, a
necessary step toward becoming farmers. This continued transition to agriculture can be seen at other sites in Iowa. The 2,800-year-old Gast Spring
site in Louisa County has the earliest unambiguous evidence of domesticated plants in the state, including squash, goosefoot, and little barley.

❋ TO VISIT

The Edgewater Park site is located north of the parking ramp of the Marriott Hotel and Conference Center, 300 E 9th Street, Coralville. Currently,

the area is empty, but it is likely to become a construction site soon; if the area is closed for construction, it can be seen from the parking ramp. On the second floor of the Marriott, there is a public display about the site that includes the excavated spear points.

✳ WANT TO LEARN MORE?

Whittaker, William E., Michael T. Dunne, Joe A. Artz, Sarah E. Horgen, and Mark L. Anderson
2007   Edgewater Park: A Late Archaic Campsite along the Iowa River. *Midcontinental Journal of Archaeology* 32:5–45.

40 Plum Grove —
Where the Rich Left the Least

✳ Iowa City, Johnson County

✳ Historic (1843–1943)

✳ SITE NUMBER 13JH311

BUILT AS THE RETIREMENT home for Robert Lucas, the first territorial governor of Iowa and the former governor of Ohio, Plum Grove is an attractive brick house on a few acres of parkland on the south side of Iowa City. When Lucas built the house in 1843, it was outside of town, a farmhouse modeled on the agrarian idyll of a gentleman farmer and statesman that dates back to the Roman era. Washington's Mount Vernon and Jefferson's Monticello epitomized the idea of the latifundia, large villa estates where learned men earned their living doing honest work, who then volunteered their time as statesmen or generals for the good of the nation when called upon. Justifiably or not, the latifundia villa was considered a cornerstone of Classical Roman democracy, and politicians in the young American democracy imitated it. Lucas was influenced by this idea.

His family members were early settlers in Ohio, and Lucas became a brigadier general in the U.S. Army prior to the War of 1812. During the war, Lucas gained renown for his calm leadership in the chaotic battles for Michigan and Detroit. After the war, he became an Ohio state senator and eventually was elected governor of Ohio in 1832. He served as chairman of the 1832 Democratic National Convention, which nominated Andrew Jackson for a second term. In 1838, he was appointed territorial governor of Iowa by President Van Buren; he was removed in 1841 after Harrison and Tyler were elected.

As territorial governor, Lucas almost brought Iowa to war with Missouri over their border in the Honey War of 1839, and he also battled with his own territorial legislators, who considered him too dictatorial. His lasting legacy was his insistence that Iowa embrace universal public education, which led to the strong public school system that survives today. After removal

Robert Lucas, first governor of the territory of Iowa, 1838–1841. From a painting by George H. Yewell made in 1865 in the possession of the State Historical Society of Iowa, Iowa City.

from office, Lucas built Plum Grove to be near the political power center at Iowa City, then the territorial and state capital, and contemplated running for governor after statehood. His declining health, reputation for irascibility, and family trouble led him to abandon his political plans, but his family remained closely connected to Iowa politics. After his death in 1853, Lucas's widow, Friendly, lived here until about 1866, when the house was sold to the Hoyt family, another politically connected family from Ohio with ties to the antislavery movement. A daughter, Eleanor Hoyt Brainerd, was born at Plum Grove and would later become a well-known author.

Jacob Carroll Switzer, also from Ohio, bought the house from the Hoyts in 1883. He was a Civil War hero who struggled financially. Plum Grove became a boardinghouse in the 1920s, when a series of increasingly poorer tenants occupied it, until it was sold to the state to become a memorial to Lucas in 1946. Beginning in 1974 and continuing until 2010, Thomas Charlton, of the University of Iowa, excavated much of the grounds around Plum Grove as part of an undergraduate field school program. The house and grounds reveal the paradox of late historical archaeology: the transformation of the economy from subsistence to consumerist in the late 19th and early 20th centuries clouds our perceptions of wealth and importance. During a century of occupation, the residents of Plum Grove became progressively poorer in terms of economic status. The Lucas family was probably among the richest in Iowa City in 1843; the Hoyts were affluent and influential; the Switzers struggled to stay middle class; and the last occupants of the house, the family of William and Winnie Hughes, were so poor they had to sell vegetables door-to-door to make ends meet during the Depression. Ironically, the majority of artifacts recovered are from the Hughes era, and as you go back in time, the quantity of artifacts decreases with each occupation, even though the occupants were wealthier and more powerful. There is only a handful of excavated artifacts that date securely to the Lucas occupation, but there are boxes and boxes of artifacts from the Hughes era. If we knew nothing about the families other than their excavated artifacts, we would be forgiven for assuming that the Lucases were the poorest occupants and that the Hughes were the richest.

The paradox is rooted in the larger economic system. There was no railroad in Iowa to bring disposable goods to the Lucas family in the 1840s, and almost all food was produced on the farm or obtained nearby, and cooked and stored in reusable containers. Essentially everything the Lucas family owned was either biodegradable, like food, clothing, and wooden items, or was rare, durable, and reusable, like stoneware crockery or metal tools. By the 1930s, the economy had transformed so much that even the poorest families regularly bought everyday items in disposable bottles and cans, and longer-lasting items like ceramic dishes and drinking glasses were inexpensive and easy to obtain. Ironically, the Hughes family came closer to starvation than the Lucas family, even though the Hughes family was virtually swimming in consumer waste.

✳ TO VISIT

Plum Grove is located just off Kirkwood Avenue in Iowa City on Carroll Street. It is open Memorial Day to October 31 in the afternoon; call to make sure it is open (319-351-5738).

✳ WANT TO LEARN MORE?

Charlton, Thomas H., Cynthia L. Otis Charlton, Stephen C. Lensink,
and James A. Sartain
1988   Historical Archaeology at Plum Grove. *Journal of the Iowa Archeological
        Society* 35:39–69.

Whittaker, William E.
1999   Production of Animal Commodities at Plum Grove, Iowa City.
        Historical Archaeology 33:44–57.

41 Jack Musgrove, Dee Norton, and Hickory Hill Park

✳ *Iowa City, Johnson County*

✳ *Woodland*

✳ SITE NUMBER 13JH1402

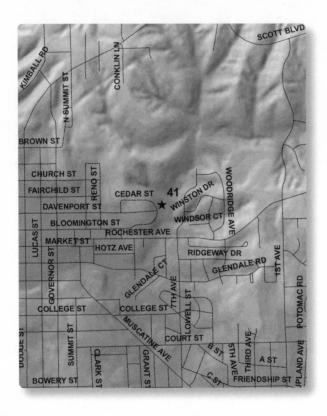

JACK MUSGROVE (1914–1980) held a deep curiosity about the cultural and natural history of Iowa. He wrote *The Waterfowl of Iowa*, still regarded as the standard book on the topic, as well as articles on the flora and fauna of Iowa. As the director of the Iowa Historical Museum and Archives in Des Moines, he helped to modernize the collections and curation of natural and historical objects. When he lived in Iowa City in the first half of the 20th century, Musgrove often liked to hike the pastures and woods of

Lily Doershuk screening at
the Dee Norton site excavations,
2011, Johnson County.

what would later become Hickory Hill Park. He noticed prehistoric Indian pottery eroding from the streambed of Ralston Creek, and over the years made a large collection, which he donated to the State Historical Society of Iowa in 1960. His location for the pottery was extremely vague — "Ralston Creek straight back of cemetery" — and it would remain hidden for another half century, as the pasture reverted to forest.

In 2011, the University of Iowa's Department of Anthropology held a field school to, among other things, attempt to locate the source of Musgrove's collection. After two weeks of frustration, a deep auger test pulled up a notched triangular arrowhead, the kind used in the terminal Late Woodland and Late Prehistoric periods. Other auger tests recovered Late Woodland ceramics, associated with a buried topsoil, that matched Musgrove's. It was not until the final days of the field school that excavation began, just enough time to confirm that there was an intact buried surface with prehistoric artifacts. The connection between the artifacts found in 2011 and Musgrove's is not perfect. Hickory Hill Park is large and might contain many sites. It is known, for example, that a small group of conical mounds was destroyed in the early 20th century near the current dam location. This new site was named for Dee Norton (1922–2009), the former chair of the University of Iowa's Department of Psychology. Like Musgrove, he also had an interest in the pasture and creeks of Hickory Hill Park, as well as all the other undeveloped areas around Iowa City. A pragmatic man who understood the complex political steps needed to acquire and preserve property to convert them into parks, he shepherded the city's political will to approve bonds to acquire the beginnings of Hickory Hill, Mercer, Willow Creek, and Terrell Mill Parks.

✳ TO VISIT

The Dee Norton site is located in Hickory Hill Park, Iowa City. Park at the south entrance, at the curve of E Bloomington Street. Hike the trail northeast to the dam; the site is located in the creek bottoms.

✳ WANT TO LEARN MORE?

Annals of Iowa
1981   Jack W. Musgrove, 1914–1980. *Annals of Iowa* 45:645–646.

Whittaker, William E.
2014   The Archaeology of Iowa City. [In press.] *Newsletter of the Iowa Archeological Society.*

Whittaker, William E., and Margaret E. Beck
2011   *Summary of the 2011 Archaeological Field Investigations at Hickory Hill Park, Iowa City, Including the Musgrove Site (13JH28), the Slavata Mound Group (13JH1332), the Pest House (13JH1398), the Dee Norton Site (13JH1402), and Sites 13JH1399 and 13JH1403.* Report on file, Department of Anthropology, University of Iowa, Iowa City.

42 Jesse Hoover—
Blacksmith and First Father

⁕ Herbert Hoover National Historic Site,
   West Branch, Cedar County

⁕ Historic (1871)

⁕ SITE NUMBER 13CD18

HERBERT HOOVER BRAGGED that he literally "bore the mark of Iowa," a brand left on his foot by a hot piece of iron he stepped on while playing barefoot at his father's blacksmith shop. It is impossible to express how proud the small town of West Branch is of Hoover, its most famous native son and our 31st president. A large portion of the town is taken over by the Herbert Hoover National Historic Site, administered by the National Park Service (NPS). Much of the small neighborhood south of downtown where the Hoovers lived and worked has been restored and rebuilt. Some of the significant original buildings are preserved, such as Herbert Hoover's birthplace cottage. Others, such as his boyhood home, are gone, while still others, such as Jesse Hoover's blacksmith shop, which was rebuilt near the original location in 1957, have been reconstructed. The NPS made every effort to re-create the neighborhood, which had almost disappeared; in the 1970s even the dirt roads that had defined this neighborhood were put back.

Jesse Hoover was a blacksmith; his shop was across the path from the small cottage where his son was born in 1874. Jesse built the shop in 1871, and a wagon shop was added in 1872. He sold the blacksmith shop in 1879 to start an implement shop on Main Street, but just a year later he died at the young age of 34. Two different smiths ran the shop before it became a veterinary clinic in 1888, and later was the site of a parsonage. After his mother died, Herbert left Iowa to live with his aunt and uncle in Oregon in 1885, but he always considered West Branch to be his hometown.

In 1970, Wilfred Husted, of the NPS, excavated a test trench to determine if the remains of Jesse Hoover's shop could be identified and if they would be affected by the proposed reconstruction of the dirt road. Finding evidence for the blacksmith shop, Husted recommended more archaeology.

Excavated Hoover blacksmith shop floor, 1970, replica blacksmith shop in background, Cedar County.

In 1971, Adrian Anderson, of the OSA, excavated its foundations, including the entire floor of the shop and large exterior areas. He and his team collected 7,684 artifacts, many of them just what one would expect to find in a blacksmith shop: hundreds of square-cut nails, worn and new horseshoes, ornate ironwork, handmade carriage bolts, and hand-wrought wagon and buggy parts. Tools of the trade included files, chisels, and cutter teeth. More personal items included a penny cut in two by a chisel, a slate pencil, and clay tobacco pipes. Some of the artifacts may have belonged to young Herbert, including clay and glass marbles and a toy tire.

A pile of old chimney bricks marked the old forge's location, and the rotting foundation logs that had been buried in place revealed the outlines of the old building. A 2-inch layer of coal indicated where the coal bin had once stood, and 1,171 horseshoe nails memorialized the countless horses that Jesse Hoover and his successors reshod here. One of the more curious findings was the base of a brick wall built on top of a log foundation on the west wall of the structure. A brick wall on top of a wooden foundation is a recipe for disaster, since the wood would soon soften and weaken the wall. An amateur mistake like that suggests Jesse Hoover built the shop himself, without professional help.

✳ TO VISIT

The Herbert Hoover National Historic Site is maintained by the NPS just south of downtown West Branch; see www.nps.gov/heho.

✳ WANT TO LEARN MORE?

Anderson, Adrian D.

1973   *The Jesse Hoover Blacksmith Shop.* Manuscript on file, Office of the State Archaeologist, University of Iowa, Iowa City.

Husted, Wilfred M.

1970   *Archaeological Test Excavations at Herbert Hoover National Historic Site, Iowa: Jesse Hoover's Blacksmith Shop and Original Penn Street.* Midwest Archaeological Center, National Park Service, Lincoln, NE.

43 Enclosures Along the Upper Iowa

✳ *Upper Iowa River, Allamakee County*

✳ *Late Prehistoric*

✳ SITE NUMBER 13AMI32

IN THE LATE PREHISTORIC PERIOD, beginning about 1,000 years ago, corn was king. The abundance of maize allowed populations to rise, causing villages to emerge, and with the appearance of larger settlements, conflict increased. No longer moving across the landscape utilizing wild resources, people needed to protect their villages, defend their territory, and define who belonged. The evidence for this transformation is visible on the landscape: Native Americans in northwest Iowa began to build walls and ditches around their villages at this time.

These enclosed settlements appeared along the Upper Iowa River, which was once known as the Oneota River and gave the prehistoric tradition its name. The Oneota people were probably the ancestors of the Chiwere Siouan–speaking tribes, including the Ioway, Otoe, and Missouria, and likely the closely related Ho-Chunk (Winnebago) as well. Their own ancestors were possibly the same Late Woodland populations that built the Effigy Mounds (47). The Oneota practiced extensive farming and built large communities, some within earthen walls and ditches. It is possible that they topped some of the earthen walls with wooden stockades. The enclosing ditches and walls might not have been defensive; they also could have been used to define membership in a tribe or clan. Those allowed within the confines are protected members of the society that built them.

Researchers have found 11 possible enclosures on the Upper Iowa River, but are not sure about the exact number because some may have been mismapped. At least five of them were destroyed before they could be properly documented. Probably more existed but suffered the same fate. The enclosures we do know about were built either on high terraces or on ridgetops overlooking the Upper Iowa. These include the Hays' Farm, Lane, Buhlman, Kumph, Ratcliffe, Lyons Farm 1 and 2, Lewis 1 and 2, New Galena, and Hartley Fort enclosures. Most were circular or nearly circular, but the New Galena earthwork is oval, and Hartley Fort, which is earlier in age and not

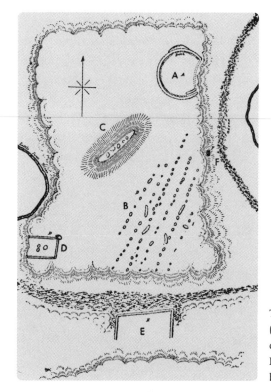

The Lane Enclosure (#A upper right) and other sites on the Upper Iowa River published by Cyrus Thomas, 1894.

Oneota, is rectangular. The size of the enclosures varied; the round ones were between 150 and 400 feet in diameter. All had evidence of ditches, and some had evidence of embankments.

Unfortunately, while several excavations have occurred at the Lane Enclosure and Hartley Fort, they were either done before the adoption of modern excavation techniques or the researchers never fully published their excavation results, so we know little about the enclosures' structures or what types of artifacts came from what types of features. As a result, we cannot begin to understand how people lived in these walled villages.

Although enclosure construction along the Upper Iowa probably ended in the protohistoric period, when disease and population shifts pushed the Oneota away from the area, there is strong evidence for one or two more ring enclosures at the Iowaville site in Van Buren County, built by the Ioway in the early 19th century, as documented by Steven De Vore and Cynthia Peterson's very recent survey (see Iowaville [27]).

✳ TO VISIT

While Hartley Fort is an Iowa State Preserve (see Woodland Mounds Preserve [25]), because of past looting at these remote sites, all of which are privately owned, their locations are confidential. The territory of the enclosures can be toured by driving along the extraordinarily scenic Iowa River Drive and the Great River Road Scenic Byway in Iowa, http://experience mississippiriver.com/. The east end is south of New Albin, off of State Highway 182, and the west end is at State Highway 76, south of Dorchester.

✳ WANT TO LEARN MORE?

Theler, James L., and Robert F. Boszhardt
2000   The End of the Effigy Mound Culture: The Late Woodland to Oneota Transition in Southwestern Wisconsin. *Midcontinental Journal of Archaeology* 25:289–312.

Tiffany, Joseph A.
1982   Hartley Fort Ceramics. *Proceedings of the Iowa Academy of Science* 89:133–150.

Whittaker, William E., and William Green
2010   Early and Middle Woodland Earthwork Enclosures in Iowa. *North American Archaeologist* 31:27–57.

44 Fish Farm Mounds

* *Allamakee County*
* *Woodland*
* SITE NUMBER 13AM100

FISH FARM MOUNDS, a cluster of 30 conical mounds, sit on a high alluvial terrace above the Mississippi floodplain at the northeast corner of Allamakee County. Twenty-eight within this group were dedicated in 1968 as one of Iowa's very first state preserves (see Woodland Mounds Preserve [25]). The remaining two mounds rest on state lands. The cluster received early attention by Cyrus Thomas of the Smithsonian Institution's Bureau of American Ethnology, who recorded this group and others nearby in the late 1800s. He noted that they ranged from 20 to 40 feet in diameter, and he described their internal soil profile and contents (his assistants opened an unknown number) as consisting of two or more burials placed adjacent to one another on the original land surface, surrounded by pottery and other artifacts, and covered with a layer of clay and then mound fill.

In 1910, brothers Ellison and Harry Orr (see Weed Park Mounds [62]) mapped the Fish Farm group and revisited the area many times over the following decades. Even in 1910, Ellison Orr reported that all but eight of the mounds remained undisturbed. On return visits to the area, he described occasional potsherds and artifacts found in the backdirt piles left by looters.

In 1968, researchers from the University of Iowa completely excavated one (#10) of the Fish Farm Mounds. No documentation of this project exists. A soils study of the mounds undertaken by Iowa State University archaeologists at the same time provided new information, including the fact that some mounds, though previously disturbed, had been restored. A Giddings hydraulic coring machine, with a 2-inch sampling tube, was used to probe a total of 20 mounds plus two locations away from the mounds on the northwest part of the terrace. The results indicated that the mounds were created from soil acquired from barrow areas relatively close by, and that the immediate environs were probably forested at the time of construction. Charcoal recovered from Mound 17 produced a radiocarbon date of A.D. 335, consistent with a Middle Woodland age.

Fish Farm Mounds, Allamakee County.

Giddings hydraulic coring machine in use at the Iowaville site, 2010, similar to that used at Fish Farm Mounds, Allamakee County.

More recent study and mapping of the mounds by David Stanley in 1987 suggest that three of the mounds, including one in the preserve, may be undisturbed, and that others, even the restored mounds, probably contain some intact portions. Others are completely gone. The larger size of some mounds, the single radiocarbon date, and the few recovered artifacts indicate a Middle Woodland age for some. Later Woodland peoples probably continued to use the site to bury and commemorate their dead.

✳ TO VISIT

The preserve is 3 miles due south of New Albin on the west side of State Highway 26. From Lansing, take Highway 26 north for 6 miles to the Fish Farm Mounds Wildlife Area, on the west side of the road (see signs). From the parking lot, climb the wooden steps to the mounds.

✳ WANT TO LEARN MORE?

Lillie, Robin M.

2002 Possible Human Bone Fragments from Fish Farm Mound Group, 13AM100, Allamakee County, Iowa. In *Reports on Iowa Burial Projects: Osteology and Archaeology*, ed. Shirley J. Schermer and Robin M. Lillie, 225–228. Research Papers 27, no. 2. Office of the State Archaeologist, University of Iowa, Iowa City.

Stanley, Lori A., and David G. Stanley

1986 *The Archeology of Allamakee County, Iowa: An Overview and Research Guide. Volume I.* HCRC #92. Highland Cultural Research Center, Highlandville, Iowa.

1988 National Register of Historic Places Nomination Form. Fish Farm Mound Group (a.k.a. Fish Farm Indian Mounds; Fish Farm Mounds State Preserve; 13AM100; Keyes Ae-26). Form on file, Office of the State Archaeologist, University of Iowa, Iowa City.

45 Nine Hundred Mounds Gone: The Great Harpers Ferry Mound Group Disappears

* Harpers Ferry, Allamakee County
* Woodland
* SITE NUMBER 13AM148

IN 1892, Theodore H. Lewis reported an astonishing find: 900 mounds in a single group—the largest collection of mounds in the world—on the terraces around Harpers Ferry. "This group consisted of 107 tailless animals, 67 birds, 98 embankments that were probably animals, 154 embankments, and 240 round mounds, the largest of which is now about 6 feet high. Total number of effigies in sight including 4 surveyed, 276. Total number of mounds including surveyed, 671. Add 229 small round mounds (estimated) that have been destroyed by cultivation makes a total of 900 mounds of all classes. All except about 50 mounds are cultivated."

Lewis was known for his careful survey of mounds—he recorded 7,767 mounds in Minnesota alone—but he made no complete map of the Harpers Ferry group, charting a handful and ignoring the rest. Because of this lack of documentation, several archaeologists have raised doubts about the legitimacy of the Harpers Ferry group. Robert Peterson critically analyzed Lewis's notes and pointed out several inconsistencies, such as the fact that he had earlier surveyed mounds in this area in 1884 and 1885 and made no mention of this enormous group. In his almost daily correspondence with Alfred Hill, he also makes no mention of the enormous group after he noted it, even though it would have been the largest he had ever seen. Later archaeologists surveying in the area mapped a handful of mounds in the Harpers Ferry area, numbers comparable to similar stretches of the river elsewhere, and they say nothing of Lewis's enormous group.

So what happened to the 900 mounds? Peterson suggests Lewis may have been dealing with a local informant who exaggerated the number, and when Lewis figured out that there were not that many mounds, he simply forgot to note that the initial count was incorrect. He may also have seen lots of small rises on the landscape and briefly considered them to be mounds,

Harpers Ferry mounds and historic gravestones, looking northeast, Allamakee County.

but then reconsidered after looking at them more carefully. Archaeologist Fred Finney thinks that many of the mounds, especially the conicals, were "mima" mounds, low rises created on river terraces made by natural forces such as stream drainage outwash depositing soil on a terrace.

Of course, it is possible that there *were* 900 mounds on the Harpers Ferry terrace; perhaps they were almost all plowed away or destroyed by development. Lewis knew mounds better than anybody, and it is unlikely that he would have described 270 effigy mounds if the mounds were predominantly conical mima mounds, but this site raises more questions than it answers.

While the total number of mounds in Harpers Ferry will never be known, there certainly were Indian mounds at the site. Charles R. Keyes noted nine mounds in the downtown area, between 1st and 2nd Streets, and excavated at least three of them in the 1930s, recovering pottery, points, and copper tools; these mounds are now gone, as are most of the other mounds that he and other archaeologists in the area mapped.

✳ TO VISIT

A small cluster of mounds in Harpers Ferry can be found on the south side of town, where an old cemetery shelters seven mounds. The cemetery is at the south end of Sandy Point Road just south of some condominiums, along the river bank. These mounds have historical graves dug into them, which is probably why they were spared destruction.

✳ WANT TO LEARN MORE?

Finney, Fred A.

2012   The Forgotten Natural Prairie Mounds of the Upper Midwest: Their Abundance, Distribution, Origin, and Archaeological Implications. In *Mima Mounds: The Case for Polygenesis and Bioturbation*, ed. Jennifer L. Horwath Burnham and Donald L Johnson, 85–133. Special Paper 490. Geological Society of America, Boulder, Colo.

Peterson, Robert W.

1986   The Strange Case of Harpers Ferry "Great Group." *Newsletter of the Iowa Archeological Society* 36(2): 3–4.

46 Paint Rock and the Lost Monolith

 ✳ *Allamakee County*

 ✳ *Protohistoric and Historic*

 ✳ SITE NUMBER 13AM87

NORTH OF THE TINY hamlet of Waukon Junction in Allamakee County, along the Mississippi bluffs, is a wide valley framed by tall cliffs. Although largely depopulated now except for a small trailer park, this area was once a Ho-Chunk (Winnebago) village; the area was destroyed by a 19th-century railroad.

The north cliff is called either Paint Rock or Painted Rock; it was an early navigation marker to steamboats. The first historical mention of Paint

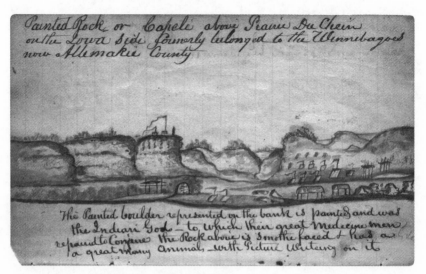

Paint Rock Bluff with village below as sketched in 1849 by William Williams, Allamakee County. Image from the Atwell Family Collection. Courtesy of Al Nelson.

Rock was in 1805 by Zebulon Pike: "Passed Painted Rock on the right of the river, 9 miles above Prairie du Chien. It has obtained this name from having numerous hieroglyphics upon it, painted by the Indians. These figures are painted on a cliff nearly perpendicular, at the height of about 25 feet from its base. Whenever the Indians pass this cliff they are in the habit of performing certain ceremonies, which their superstition leads them to believe efficacious in rendering any enterprise in which they may be engaged successful."

In 1823, C. J. Beltrami, an Italian, mentioned the rocks while traveling up the river: "Nine miles above the Prairie, at a point where the savages pay their adoration to a rock which they annually paint with red and yellow." French traders called Paint Rock *Roche Peinte* or *Rochers Peints*. There had been a Ho-Chunk village here in 1838, as mentioned in correspondence of the Commission of Indian Affairs. In 1827, a family of French Métis were killed here while trading with Indians.

In 1849, William Williams sketched this location. This sketch is part of the Atwell family collection, one of 88 he drew on his 1849 trip up the Mississippi and around Michigan. Al Nelson, of Fort Dodge, has been investigating the subjects of these sketches. One of the drawings shows an

Paint Rock bluff, Allamakee County.

apparently abandoned Indian village in the foreground, with the bluffs in the background. The south bluffs are painted, and flags fly above this bluff. In the foreground, near the Indian village, Williams drew a tall wide rock and wrote: "Painted Rock, or Capila, above Prairie du Chien, on the Iowa side formerly belonging to the Winnebagos, now Allamakee County. The painted boulder represented on the bank is painted and was the Indian God—to which their great medicine men repaired to conjure. The rock is smooth faced and has a great many animals with picture writing on it." He noted in his journal, "Allamakee & Winneshiek Counties was the great settlement, also Clayton Co., of the Indians. Passed here Capila Rock where there stands a singular rock, an Indian God painted up by the Indians & worshipped by them, the Capila Mound or Rock stands a short distance above on the Iowa side." A second sketch shows this painted monolith. It is not clear from his crude sketch on which bank of the Mississippi he was standing.

   Why Williams used the name "Capila" for the bluff is also unknown; perhaps he was confusing it with the "Cap-a-l'ail" (Garlic Cape) bluffs, which are about 20 miles north. "Cap-a-l'ail" was shortened to "Capoli" in later accounts; Elliott Coues discussed common confusion over the names of various bluffs in the area in his notes in the book *Expeditions of Zebulon Montgomery Pike.*

In 1911, Ellison Orr made the first systematic survey of Paint Rock. He found several petroglyphs engraved on the sandstone cliff, along with hundreds of vertical lines. Above these images he encountered smeared splotches of red, remnants of rock painting. Orr made no mention of the large smooth-faced monolith along the bank that earlier travelers had noted.

What was this large rock along the bank? There are historical accounts of Indians of the region revering painted boulders. In 1855, James H. Lockwood, an early settler at Prairie du Chien, wrote, "On the prairies are often found isolated granite rocks, which, from their isolated and scattered appearance, are considered holy, and every Indian who passes them either paints them with vermilion or leaves a piece of tobacco as a tribute. Hence the great number of places in this country where the Sioux were accustomed to pass that bear the name of Painted Rock." Henry Schoolcraft noted a smaller one near Cass Lake in Minnesota, painted red with offerings left nearby; the local Indian name for these rocks was *Shingaba Wossin,* which translates as "image stone."

✴ TO VISIT

Much of the Paint Rock bluffs are part of Yellow River State Forest. To see the bluffs, take the Great River Road (State Highway 364) to Waukon Junction. Paint Rock Road runs between the two bluffs. Nobles Island to the east, opposite the south bluff, is state-owned and provides an approximate view of the bluffs from Williams's perspective.

✴ WANT TO LEARN MORE?

Nelson, Alan F.

2012   Major William Williams' Excursion: Espionage or Adventure? *Journal of the Early Americas* 11:6–12.

Orr, Ellison J.

1920 The Painted Rock Enlarged Crevice. Manuscript on file, Office of the State Archaeologist, University of Iowa, Iowa City.

Williams, William

1920 Major William Williams' Journal of a Trip to Iowa in 1849. *Annals of Iowa* 12:242–281.

47 The Beauty of Effigy Mounds

* *Effigy Mounds National Monument, Allamakee and Clayton Counties*
* *Archaic–Late Prehistoric*
* SITE NUMBER 13AM189

WHEN SOLDIERS FROM Fort Crawford (1816–1831) in Prairie du Chien led patrols into the interior of what is now Iowa, they crossed the Mississippi River on skiffs and marched up a steep valley slot to the top of the bluff. Here, their trail curved around Paleozoic rock formations and led to a high vista, where they could see dozens of miles up and down the Mississippi valley. This military trail, which exists to this day, led them along a curious line of earthen mounds that seemed to be shaped like animals, including 10 bears and three birds. Like the soldiers, the bears appeared to be marching single file along the bluff.

The Marching Bears are the best-known feature of Effigy Mounds National Monument, but they are only a small part of Iowa's premiere archaeological destination. Founded in 1949 after a half century of lobbying by state leaders and the "founding fathers" of Iowa archaeology, Ellison Orr and Charles R. Keyes (see Weed Park Mounds [62]), Effigy Mounds includes more than 200 prehistoric mounds; about half are in the Sny Magill Unit several miles south of McGregor (discussed below [49]), the rest are spread out along the bluffs and terraces on both sides of the mouth of the Yellow River.

Although Effigy Mounds National Monument is famous for its bird and bear effigies, the majority of mounds are actually conical (round) in shape, including a long string of 18 evenly spaced conicals on a narrow ridge sticking out into the Mississippi valley on Fire Point. Others are linear in shape, and some are "compound," strings of conicals connected by linears like pearls on a necklace. The Late Woodland animal-shaped effigy mounds are found in a small region of the United States, mostly in southern Wisconsin, but extending into nearby areas in Iowa and Minnesota.

Most of the mounds at Effigy Mounds were damaged by looters prior to the establishment of the park. After the monument was founded, the National Park Service led several mound excavations and determined that the mounds were likely built as burial places for Native Americans, and that most of the mounds date to the Late Woodland period, including all of the effigy mounds. Excavation has not been allowed in the mounds since the early 1970s. Other sites at Effigy Mounds include large village sites along the Mississippi, probably inhabited by the builders of the mounds, which have only been partially explored archaeologically. Other sites indicate occupations from the Archaic to the Late Prehistoric periods. Several Indian tribes with deep ties to the region act as stewards of the mounds.

An ongoing discussion is how to maintain the mounds. Historically, and probably prehistorically, the bluffs did not have large trees, meaning that the mounds were visible up and down the Mississippi valley for miles. Removal of the woods surrounding the mounds would be difficult and expensive, and would have to be done carefully to not damage the mounds.

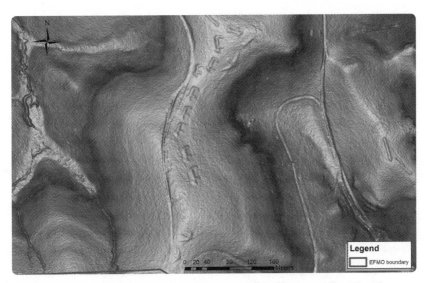

Shaded relief map created from lidar image, Marching Bear Group, Effigy Mounds National Monument, Clayton County. Image courtesy of Albert LeBeau, produced by Effigy Mounds National Monument Cultural Resources, U.S. National Park Service.

✳ TO VISIT

Effigy Mounds National Monument is located a few miles north of McGregor on State Highway 76: www.nps.gov/efmo (563-873-3491 ext. 202). The park no longer charges admission, but it is good to check in at the visitor center. The center has displays of artifacts and frequently shows an interpretive film on Effigy Mounds.

The monument is divided into three parts. Sny Magill is remote, and discussed below (49). The main part of the park is divided into north and south units, on either side of the Yellow River. The trail system within Effigy Mounds is extensive; to walk to the farthest mounds at Hanging Rock, which has arguably the most scenic view in all of Iowa, it is about 3.5 miles from the visitor center. The less adventurous can enjoy the mounds near the visitor center, or walk up the steep bluff for a quick hike to see the Little Bear and Great Bear mound groups.

At this time there is no easy way to walk to the south unit from the visitor center; there is parking along State Highway 76 south of the Yellow River, and a trail entrance across the road. The Marching Bears are at the very end of the trail, about 2.5 miles south of the entrance. All trails are well maintained and marked, but hiking boots are recommended because the bluff trails can be steep. Please stay on the trails and do not walk on the mounds.

✳ WANT TO LEARN MORE?

Birmingham, Robert A., and Amy L. Rosebrough
2003 On the Meaning of Effigy Mounds. *Wisconsin Archeologist* 84:21–36.

Lenzendorf, Dennis
2000 *Effigy Mounds: A Guide to Effigy Mounds National Monument.* Fort Washington, PA: Eastern National.

National Park Service
1999 *Effigy Mounds National Monument: Timeless Treasure.* Washington, D.C.: National Park Service, Department of the Interior.

Orr, Ellison J.
1917 Notable Mound Groups in and near the Proposed Government Park at McGregor. *Proceedings of the Iowa Academy of Science* 24:43–46.

48 Pike's Peak — Mounds and the Unconstructed Fort

✳ *Clayton County*

✳ *Woodland*

✳ SITE NUMBER 13CT59

IN 1805, FAMED EXPLORER Zebulon Pike set out to explore the Upper Mississippi; among his duties was to find a location suitable for a military fort near the mouth of the Wisconsin River, then the main trading route from the Mississippi River to the Great Lakes. Pike strongly recommended a high bluff promontory across the Mississippi from the mouth of the Wisconsin River because it had a sweeping view of the entire valley, including the trading hamlet of Prairie du Chien and the Wisconsin delta. A fort built up there would be impervious to attack — the bluffs were nearly vertical, and the top was so high that musket fire from below would be ineffective.

The U.S. Army had a different idea and chose to place the fort, named Fort Shelby, on Brisbois Island, closer to Prairie du Chien. This proved to be a foolish decision. A small group of British soldiers and allied Indians had no trouble shelling the fort into submission during the War of 1812. This defeat would not have happened if the fort had been built on the bluffs on the Iowa side, and the United States probably would not have lost control of the Upper Mississippi in the war. Much of the Pike's Peak bluff land was purchased by Alexander McGregor, the founder of the town of McGregor, who claimed he was a descendant of the fabled Scots hero Rob Roy. His grand-niece Martha Buell Munn donated the property to the federal government in 1919, probably as part of the early efforts to establish what later became Effigy Mounds National Monument (47). The federal government transferred the property to Iowa in 1936. Soon people working for the Works Progress Administration's employment programs made improvements to the new state park.

Although regrettable from a military standpoint, the lack of a fort on the high bluffs below what is now McGregor helped to preserve a remarkable collection of mounds. In 1912, Ellison Orr mapped 55 mounds in seven groups along the bluffs, including 7 effigy, 38 conical, and 10 linear and compound mounds. Clark Mallam and John Hotopp resurveyed these mound groups in 1973 and 1978, respectively. Although Mallam found four new mound groups with 14 new mounds, both researchers noted that most of the mounds mapped by Orr had been disturbed or destroyed by looting, farming, and construction.

In 1983, Mallam returned to Pike's Peak and used aerial photography to photograph the mounds, outlined with lime powder. Mallam's work was part of a larger program to document mounds of northeast Iowa using lime and airplanes; in the 1970s and early 1980s he led large crews of volunteers to trace hundreds of mounds with lime and to oversee their photography. Luther College holds hundreds of his photos.

✳ TO VISIT

Pike's Peak State Park is on the bluffs just south of McGregor. From McGregor, follow the Great River Road (Walton Street) south up the bluff to Pike's Peak Road. Follow the signs.

✳ WANT TO LEARN MORE?

Mallam, R. Clark

1976   *The Iowa Effigy Mound Manifestation: An Interpretive Model.* Report 9. Office of the State Archaeologist, University of Iowa, Iowa City.

1982   Ideology from the Earth: Effigy Mounds in the Midwest. *Archaeology* 35(4): 60-64.

1984   The Pikes Peak Start Project: Mounds and "Sacred Space." *Newsletter of the Iowa Archeological Society* 109:7–9.

Mallam, R. Clark, E. Arthur Bettis III, and Robert W. Petersen

1979   An Archaeological Reconnaissance Survey of Pikes Peak State Park. Luther College Archaeological Research Center, Decorah, Iowa.

49 Sny Magill — A Glimpse of What May Have Been

✳ Sny Magill Unit, Effigy Mounds National
Monument, Clayton County

✳ Archaic and Woodland

✳ SITE NUMBER 13CT18

WHEN THEODORE H. LEWIS surveyed mound groups in the upper Midwest in the 1880s and 1890s, he recorded the location of more than 10,000 mounds. The farther north he went, the more mounds he found; in Minnesota alone he recorded 7,767. While it is possible that Indians in Minnesota built more mounds than people in Iowa or other states did, a more reasonable explanation is that less land in Minnesota was plowed in the late 19th century than in other parts of the Midwest. Even now, much of Minnesota does not have good soil or climate for farming, and much of the land is too hilly to plow.

By the time Lewis made his surveys, almost every inch of Iowa was under plow, and most of the few surviving mound groups he recorded were on virtually inaccessible bluffs, ridges, and terraces, spots where it was not worth the trouble to plow. While mound groups in Minnesota can include hundreds of mounds at a single site, in Iowa, the largest known mound group is Sny Magill, now part of Effigy Mounds National Monument (47). When Lewis mapped Sny Magill in 1885, he recorded 94 mounds. Subsequent surveys identified several other possible mounds nearby, bringing the total to as many as 121, but researchers debate whether the smallest mounds are human-made or natural. Sny Magill contains two bird effigies, three bear effigies, and five linear mounds; the rest are conical mounds. Excavation in the 1960s revealed that the mound group was built mostly in the Late Woodland period, but some of the mounds are probably older, dating to the Late Archaic to Early Woodland transition.

Large mound sites in the bottom of a floodplain are uncommon in the Midwest. Flood deposits can bury mounds, and the soils in a floodplain are often rich and easily accessible, so they are usually farmed. Why was Sny

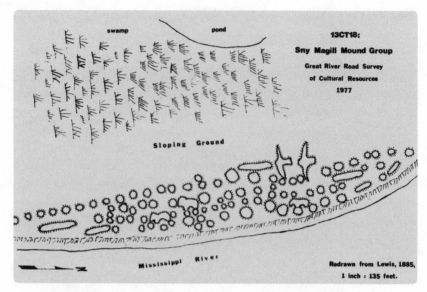

Theodore H. Lewis's 1885 map of the Sny Magill mound group, Clayton County.

Magill spared, when so many other mounds disappeared under the plow before Lewis could survey them? The site stands on a gravel bar along the edge of the Mississippi, and it floods less frequently than other parts of the floodplain, so it was not buried in silt. The site was difficult to get to, almost an island, and there were no adjacent areas suitable for farming.

The 100 or so mounds at Sny Magill may be a remnant of what was: dozens or hundreds of mounds in a group, with groups clustered up and down major river bottoms. Within a few decades after Euroamerican settlement began in the 1830s, almost all of these mounds disappeared, unknown and unmapped.

✳ TO VISIT

Sny Magill is part of Effigy Mounds National Monument, which is north of Marquette, 151 Highway 76, Harpers Ferry (563-873-3491). First check in at Effigy Mounds National Monument to learn whether Sny Magill is open — it is closed during high water. The site itself is south of Marquette, just off the Great River Road (Highway 76).

Flags marking surveyed
mounds, Sny Magill mound
group, Clayton County.

South end of the Sny Magill mound group, 1980, Clayton County. Photo by Judy or
Clark Mallam, Courtesy of Luther College, Decorah.

✳ WANT TO LEARN MORE?

Beaubien, Paul L.

1953   Cultural Variation within Two Woodland Mound Groups of Northeastern Iowa. *American Antiquity* 19:56–66.

Lenzendorf, Dennis

2000   *Effigy Mounds: A Guide to Effigy Mounds National Monument*. Fort Washington, PA: Eastern National.

Whittaker, William E., and Glenn R. Storey

2008   Ground-Penetrating Radar Survey of the Sny Magill Mound Group, Effigy Mounds National Monument, Iowa. *Geoarchaeology* 23:474–499.

50 Dragoon Life at Fort Atkinson

* Fort Atkinson, Winneshiek County
* Historic (1840–1849)
* SITE NUMBER 13WH57

IN THE EARLY 19TH CENTURY, the Sauk and Dakota were arch-enemies, fighting over territory and raiding each other's camps. These conflicts threatened the stability of the western frontier, so the U.S. government intervened and in 1825 drew the Neutral Line across the northern part of what is now Iowa. The Sauk were supposed to stay south of it, and the Dakota were supposed to stay north of it. In reality, the line was not marked on the ground and the United States had no real military presence, so the fighting continued. In 1830, the U.S. government expanded the boundary by creating a Neutral Zone, a buffer 20 miles on either side of the Neutral Line where neither tribe was allowed.

After the 1832 Black Hawk War and the massacre at Bad Axe, Wisconsin, when hundreds of Sauk were killed by the army and affiliated tribes, the U.S. government decided to remove all tribes east of the Mississippi to reservations west of that river. A problem arose: where to put all the tribes? Unfortunately for the Ho-Chunk (Winnebago) of Wisconsin, the government decided in 1832 to stick them into the Neutral Ground, between their longtime enemy the Dakota and the Sauk, with whom they had an icy relationship. Early attempts at removal proved unsuccessful; most Ho-Chunk refused to move, and those forced to move soon slipped back into Wisconsin.

Fort Atkinson was built near the center of the Neutral Ground in 1840 to keep peace between tribes, to force the Ho-Chunk to stay in Iowa, and to prevent U.S. settlers from entering until the area could be formally opened for settlement. Situated on a bluff of Roberts Creek, a tributary of the Turkey River, the fort was a lonely outpost where desertion, drunkenness, and fighting were common among soldiers. For much of its history, mounted dragoon soldiers based here patrolled northern Iowa, enforcing an unworkable policy. In 1843, the army removed the Sauk from Iowa, and by 1849 the Ho-Chunk were gone as well.

Lieutenant A. Reynolds's 1842 sketch of Fort Atkinson, Winneshiek County.

Foundations of excavated western barracks, facing north, Fort Atkinson State Preserve, Winneshiek County.

The abandoned fort is one of the most picturesque places in Iowa, and the only place in the state where you can find a frontier fort with original buildings in their original location. The grounds are surrounded by a stockade that was rebuilt in 2006, but most of the buildings on the grounds are original, including the north barracks, the southwest blockhouse, and the powder house. The northeast blockhouse was extensively rebuilt and cannot be considered original. The foundations of most of the other fort buildings are exposed on the ground surface; these were excavated in the early 1940s by Sigurd Reque, a professor from Luther College. Reque did not keep notes or make maps of his excavations. The artifacts he dug up were sorted only by the building from which they came. When a catalog was made of them 25 years later, it was realized that most of the artifacts postdated the fort period, and the nicer military artifacts were missing. In 1966, the University of Iowa excavated six latrines and a bake house. The latrine contents revealed that the officers of Fort Atkinson had a comparatively luxuriant life, with English ceramics, French olive oil, German marbles, pipes, dominoes, musical instruments, and liquor bottles. In 2005 and 2006, much of the grounds were surveyed with ground-penetrating radar, finding new foundations and features. Test excavations prior to the reconstruction of the stockade in 2006 revealed more of the daily life of soldiers, including a root cellar.

✳ TO VISIT

Historic Fort Atkinson is an Iowa state preserve and is listed on the National Register of Historic Places as a Historic District. It is located at 303 2nd Street NW, Fort Atkinson. Just follow the signs. The grounds are open during daylight, and admission is free. The fort has a museum, located in the north barracks, with artifacts and dioramas. A public museum connected to the city library, just southeast of the fort, contains additional artifacts and information. The best time to visit is during the last full weekend of September, when costumed buckskinners, musket men, and traders camp around the fort for the annual Rendezvous Days, with craft sales, reenactments, and historical displays.

✳ WANT TO LEARN MORE?

Carr, Jeffery T., and William E. Whittaker
2009 Fort Atkinson, Iowa, 1840–1849. In *Frontier Forts of Iowa: Indians, Traders, and Soldiers, 1682–1862*, ed. William E. Whittaker, 146–160. Iowa City: University of Iowa Press.

51 The Hewitt-Olmsted Trading Post

* Winneshiek County
* Historic (1840–1848)
* SITE NUMBER 13WH160

WHEN THE HO-CHUNK (Winnebago) were forced out of Wisconsin and into Iowa in 1840, one of the compensations was direct annuity payments, paid by the U.S. government every fall. A whole industry of white traders emerged to take advantage of the annuity payments, building temporary camps, usually licensed by the government, to sell Indians everything from guns to cloth to whiskey at inflated prices. Most left as soon as the money ran out, but a few were more permanent operations, places where traders extended credit to Indians and Indians often lived nearby. One of these permanent locations is known as the Hewitt-Olmsted Trading Post, located a few miles south of Fort Atkinson along Goddard Creek.

The dates of the post are unknown, but it was active sometime during the period when the Ho-Chunk lived in Iowa, 1840–1849. The main proprietor of the post was David Olmsted, although there are historical suggestions that Joseph Hewitt worked as Olmsted's partner or started the post and sold it to Olmsted. Olmstead learned Ho-Chunk language and customs, and was apparently trusted by his Indian customers. Five log buildings stood at the post: two large houses, a store, a storage house, and a blacksmith shop. The Ho-Chunk had a camp and farmed a few acres nearby. They had a small cemetery near the creek, and one of their chiefs may have been buried there.

After the Ho-Chunk left Iowa in 1849, the post property was sold to Josiah Goddard Sr. in 1850, and became part of a farm. The blacksmith shop and store still were standing in 1877, and the foundation of one of the buildings was reused in a building in the 1920s. Olmstead later became the mayor of St. Paul, Minnesota. For a while in the 20th century, a small park was maintained at the site, with a reconstructed cabin built on an old foundation. This cabin fell into disrepair and was demolished.

In 1999, Alan Becker, a local history teacher, led students in an investigation of the post's history and site. With the help of archaeologist Cynthia Peterson, his students mapped the area and excavated 17 test units. Survey of the post site revealed that many of the original limestone foundations were visible in the ground, as were suggestive depressions where buildings probably once stood. Artifacts recovered included a trade bead, a brass finger ring, a jewelry clasp, clay pipe fragments, a Jew's harp, knives, and part of a flintlock rifle; these artifacts helped to confirm the location of the trading post.

Later research provided more information. Detailed Iowa Department of Natural Resources topographic mapping of the area using lidar in 2009 revealed suggestive rows in the lower terrace to the north, perhaps indications that Indians had once farmed here. Currently, the site is under threat from a small, but growing, quarrying operation to the east; we do not know if the site extends to the quarry area. In 2010, the Archaeological Conservancy, a national nonprofit organization dedicated to acquiring and preserving American archaeological sites, recognized the importance of the trading post and purchased the site.

☀ TO VISIT

The site is located along State Highway 24 southwest of Fort Atkinson. The land is owned by the Archaeological Conservancy, which, at this time, wants to preserve the site by keeping people out. Many of the artifacts from the trading post are on display at the Fort Atkinson Museum, part of the Fort Atkinson library (see Fort Atkinson [50]).

☀ WANT TO LEARN MORE?

McConaughy, Josh
2011   A Glimpse of the American Frontier. *Newsletter of the Iowa Archeological Society* 61(1): 6.

Peterson, Cynthia L., and Alan C. Becker
2001   *Neutral Ground Archaeology: GIS Predictive Modeling, Historic Document Microfilm Indexing, and Field Investigations at 1840s-Era Sites in Winneshiek County, Iowa.* Contract Completion Report 805. Office of the State Archaeologist, University of Iowa, Iowa City.

52 The Elgin Brewery

* Elgin, Fayette County
* Historic (1871–1888)
* SITE NUMBER 13FT125

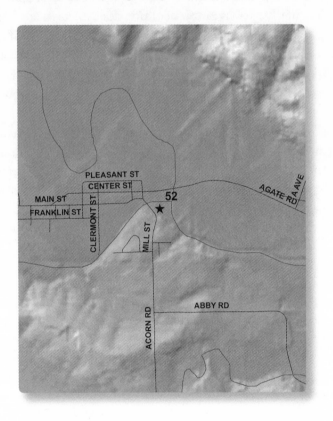

WHILE GERMAN-STYLE beers dominate the American beer market now, German brewers were a relatively late addition to the American brewing scene, arriving in numbers only in the mid-19th century. The immigration of Germans, some 127,000 to Iowa by 1890, made breweries an important part of the state's economy and culture. In 1884, there were 111 breweries in 66 Iowa counties. Recent investigations at the Elgin Brewery, one of only two in Iowa that have been studied archaeologically, add to our knowledge of the structure and function of these businesses and the lives of the brewers themselves.

The Elgin Brewery, also known as the Schori & Lehman Brewery, was the first such enterprise in the town. Historians attribute its construction to immigrants Casper Schneider, from Switzerland, and Lewis Thoma, from Germany. It was soon acquired by Nicolas Schori, who operated it with his brother-in-law, Fred Lehman. Built between 1871 and 1873, the brewery stood south of Otter Creek and west of the Turkey River at the south edge of town. Buildings still standing at the site include a well-preserved 1870s malt house and a brick home built for the Schori family in 1878. Although the historical records are somewhat ambiguous, the brewery apparently remained in operation until 1888, four years after Iowa enacted statewide prohibition.

The malt house was a square, two-story, brick-and-stone structure used for converting cereal grains into malt. This process starts by soaking barley in water to force germination and then drying the grain with hot air. Constructed with thick, limestone walls, the malt house's ground floor banked into the bluff slope, and its flat, concrete floor sank into the ground 2 feet below the door sill. This configuration suggests the need for a steady, cool temperature year-round, as well as a clean, paved drying surface to spread out the soaked grain. The upper story offered a dry, safe area to store the barley, less accessible to rodents. A circular stone-lined well that provided a reliable source of water for all stages of the brewing process still exists close to both the malt house and the main brewery building.

Archaeological investigation at the Elgin Brewery by Tallgrass Historians, L.C., in 2007–2008 revealed remnants of two intact stone and brick foundations and a portion of the foundation or cellar of the main brewery building itself. Associated artifacts included fragments of period items used in the home such as ceramics, crockery, bottles, glass, and lamp glass, as well as metal hardware, wire nails, and masonry fragments probably associated with the brewery. Ceramic buttons, leather shoe/boot fragments, a slate pencil, and a clay smoking pipe were probably personal items lost or discarded.

According to project director Leah Rogers, the Elgin Brewery is an exceptionally well preserved example of a pre-prohibition brewery. An illustration of the property appears in the *Andreas Illustrated Historical Atlas*, published in 1875, not long after the brewery was built. This resource offers historic archaeologists and architectural historians the occasional opportunity to

Elgin Brewery and associated buildings, *Andreas Atlas*, 1875, Fayette County.

Elgin Brewery malt house today, Fayette County. Photo by Leah D. Rogers, courtesy of Tallgrass Historians, L.C., Iowa City.

"see" what the 19th-century farmstead or building they are researching actually looked like. The depiction of the Elgin Brewery shows the main building with an office or house to its right—perhaps the original house on the property. The main brewery appears to have a frame superstructure, many windows, and a steep, sloping roof. Rogers suggests that the malt house is either not accurately depicted in the illustration or may be hidden behind the main building. It may also have been added in 1878, when the Schori home was built, but after the atlas was published.

✳ TO VISIT

Elgin is located on the eastern edge of Fayette County in northeastern Iowa. Major routes to the area are: Highway 18 from Madison, Wisconsin, to Iowa W51, south to Elgin. From Cedar Rapids, take Highway 13 north to Elkader. Take Highway 56 west to the Elgin turnoff on W55. The existing brewery structures are located on the south edge of Elgin: www.elginiowa.org.

✳ WANT TO LEARN MORE?

Rogers, Leah D.

1996 *"It Was Some Brewery": Data Recovery of the City Brewery Site, 13PK661, Des Moines, Iowa.* Mount Vernon, Iowa: Leah D. Rogers.

2008 *Schori-Lehmann House and Brewery Malt House: Update Historical/ Architectural Survey, City of Elgin, Fayette County, Iowa.* Iowa City, Iowa: Tallgrass Historians, L.C.

2013 History and Archaeology of the Elgin Brewery Site, Fayette County, Iowa. *Journal of the Iowa Archeological Society* 60:1–5.

53 The Ruins of Motor Town

* *Clayton County*
* Historic (1868–1883)
* SITE NUMBER 13CT193

THE IMPOSING MOTOR MILL was a colossal monument, six stories tall with 5-feet-thick stone walls. At 90 feet, it was one of the tallest buildings in the state for its time. Built in 1868–1869, it required the labor of scores of stonemasons and quarrymen and cost $90,000; adjusted for inflation, this would be about $1.5 million in 2014.

Unfortunately, the Motor Mill was never very successful. Wheat crops were poor when it was completed, so it did not mill much flour, its primary function. A planned expansion into milling wool did not happen because of a lack of investors. An adjacent town was platted in 1875, but it did not grow beyond a few houses, a store, a school, a tavern, stables, and an ice house. Locals applied for a post office, but it never appeared. A proposed narrow-gauge railroad was never built, because the Turkey River flooded too often at the chosen location. The 1886 Clayton County plat book has an ambitious map of the Motor town plat, with about 200 lots laid out in the floodplain east of the mill, but it showed that the town had only three buildings. In the end, a flood in 1883 wrecked the mill's mechanism. The Motor townsite faded away, and the old mill became farm buildings.

In 1984, archaeologists excavated parts of the site, trying to find a way to rebuild the Motor bridge and modernize the road. A test unit at the suspected site of the town's 1867 general store found no evidence of a structure, but historical accounts suggested that it might have been at a different location. Archaeologists did find and excavate a barn associated with the store, but it contained few artifacts.

A nearby site in the abandoned town area yielded evidence of two houses. Intriguingly, a prehistoric scatter of artifacts is also in this area. When archaeologists excavated in 1984, they suspect they encountered the base of a truncated mound, possibly the only time a mound has been discovered within an excavation in Iowa.

Perhaps the most interesting find were the remains of the funicular cable car system used to lower rock from the quarry near the bluff top. Two cars were attached to a long rope, and the weight of the stone in the descending car pulled up the empty car. The stone embankment wall and ramp for this railway are still visible.

✸ TO VISIT

The mill still stands and is a local landmark occasionally open for tours; see motormill.org. The Motor townsite is located about 7 miles southeast of Elkader; take Iowa Highway 13 to C1X (Grape Road) about 4 miles. At the top of a hill, turn south on Galaxy. Continue 3 miles to Motor Mill.

The same funicular principle used at the Motor townsite is used in the famous Fenlon Place Elevator in Dubuque, where a cable pulls cars up and down the bluffs; open daily at 512 Fenelon Place (top) or on 4th Street, just off Bluff Street (bottom).

✸ WANT TO LEARN MORE?

Rogers, Leah D., and David G. Stanley
1984   *Final Report of Phase II Investigations at the Motor Townsite, Clayton County, Iowa, 13CT193/194, 196-199.* HCRC #35. Highland Cultural Research Center, Highlandville, Iowa.

54 Death and the Turkey River
Mound Group

✳ *Clayton County*

✳ *Archaic and Woodland*

✳ SITE NUMBER 13CTI

MANY NATIVE AMERICAN groups feared the dead. Ethnohistorical accounts describe the uneasy relationship between the living and the deceased. While dead ancestors could intervene on behalf of the living, some Indians also believed that the spirits of the dead could be malevolent, the ghost of an ancestor could be displeased, or the spirit of an enemy might seek revenge. Spirits themselves might need protection. The graves of a revered ancestor might need to be shielded from spells or curses, so that the dead might remain benevolent or at peace.

Robert L. Hall studied many of the beliefs about the afterlife among Native Americans, and he found some common themes among disparate groups. Water was often seen as a barrier to spirits; the dead could not cross water. The Omaha believed that a person could evade a pursuing ghost by crossing a stream or river. In some cultures the dead were buried on the other side of a river from the village, to provide a barrier against ghosts. Circles, like water, were also barriers, because they can enclose the dead or keep the dead out. If a powerful person died and his or her spirit was feared, the living might encircle the grave with a ditch to contain the ghost; conversely, survivors might encircle the burial of a beloved person to protect it from malice.

You can see such encircled graves at the Turkey River mound group, which contains 41 mounds on a bluff overlooking the mouth of the Turkey River. They date from the Late Archaic to the Late Woodland period. At one end of the mound group is a large ring ditch about 325 × 230 feet in diameter, 12 feet wide, and 18 inches deep. This ring encircles one large, badly damaged mound and two smaller mounds. Marshall McKusick excavated many of the mounds here in the 1960s. He found that the mounds inside the ring contained burials that were fairly typical of the Woodland period;

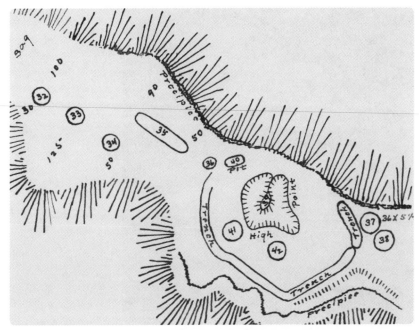

Turkey River mounds as sketched by Ellison Orr. Photo courtesy of the State Historical Society of Iowa, Iowa City, Charles R. Keyes Archaeological Collection, and the University of Iowa Office of the State Archaeologist.

they were covered with a thick layer of red ocher, but otherwise had no grave goods.

Mounds 37 and 38, just outside the ring, however, contained some very unusual burials. Mound 37 contained a headless skeleton encircled by a ring of large limestone rocks. If the people who constructed this grave believed that circles would contain supernatural power, this individual must have been very powerful. The stone ring would have protected the individual's spirit from malice or protected others from his or her spirit. Excavators also found a bone tube, probably made from a human tibia, in this mound; its significance is unknown.

Mound 38 was even more unusual; it contained at least 11 individuals. One individual, also headless, was buried below a pile of rock slabs in the center of the mound. Buried with him were the remains of an adolescent and young child. In the young child's mouth were 32 shell beads. To the southeast of the mound center were six individuals, four without heads,

Transit and plane table, mapping tools used at the Turkey River mound group, 1964, Clayton County.

buried in a common pit. In addition to being headless, many of the skeletons showed evidence of violence that occurred at the time of death or after death. One had a stone arrowhead in its ribs. One had a large, long, copper dagger jammed into its body at the base of its neck. One had a large ceremonial blade placed where its head should be. These do not seem like the bodies of enemies: they were buried with care, sprinkled with ocher, and provided with grave goods, including a stone bar amulet.

Ultimately, this site raises more questions than it answers. Why was there such a difference between the treatment of the dead inside and outside the ditch enclosure? Were the ditch and the stone ring enclosures meant to contain the dead buried within, were they meant to protect them, or did they have some other meaning? Why are so many of the dead headless? Were the heads removed by their families as part of a ritual, as is known from some historical Indian accounts? Who caused the violence? The burial site must have been an extremely potent location to whomever built it, fraught with supernatural powers that, ultimately, only they understood.

✳ TO VISIT

Turkey River Mounds State Preserve is located south of Guttenberg; take the Great River Road (U.S. Highway 52) and turn east on Estes Point Road. Tampering with burial mounds is a state crime with serious consequences (see Old Pacific City Cemetery [14]).

✳ WANT TO LEARN MORE?

Green, William, and Shirley J. Schermer
1988   The Turkey River Mound Group. In *Archaeological and Paleo-environmental Studies in the Turkey River Valley, Northeastern Iowa*, ed. William Green, 131–198. Research Papers 12, no. 1. Office of the State Archaeologist, University of Iowa, Iowa City.

Hall, Robert L.
1976   Ghosts, Water Barriers, Corn, and Sacred Enclosures in the Eastern Woodlands. *American Antiquity* 41:360–364.

Herzberg, Ruth, and John A. Pearson
2001   *The Guide to Iowa's State Preserves*. Iowa City: University of Iowa Press.

McKusick, Marshall
1964   Exploring Turkey River Mounds. *Palimpsest* 55:473–486.

55 Four Mounds
Survive the Odds

✳ *Dubuque, Dubuque County*

✳ *Woodland*

✳ SITE NUMBER 13DB21

ALONG THE BLUFF EDGE on the far north side of Dubuque, four low mounds remain. Their survival is an accident; they were built on a bluff ridge that was too narrow to farm, so they were spared the most common fate of mounds, the slow erosion under steel blades. The Burden family purchased the land in 1906 and built a mansion near the mounds on a 52-acre parcel. The Mission-Prairie–style mansion was accompanied by a colonial-style home, servants' quarters, a carriage house, and other buildings, including a ski jump. Because of their wealth and love of the outdoors, the Burdens maintained the area as parkland surrounded by wilderness.

J. C. Collier, a local resident, first noted the mounds in 1924, and he corresponded with Charles R. Keyes (see Weed Park Mounds [62]); Collier observed that the mounds had been looted. Archaeologist Anton Till visited the mounds in 1977 and noted that they were well maintained as part of the estate grounds.

When Elizabeth Burden died in 1982, she willed the estate to the city of Dubuque. Unable to fund the park or maintain the buildings because of budget cuts during the Farm Crisis, the city of Dubuque tried to give the site back to the Burden descendants in 1987. Two of Elizabeth's grandsons teamed up with the Iowa Natural Heritage Foundation to create the Four Mounds Foundation, which obtained a 99-year lease for the property from the city for $1. The estate is now maintained as a bed and breakfast along with an event center and nature trails.

The mounds were listed on the National Register of Historic Places in 2000. In 2008, archaeologists surveyed the grounds surrounding them and found five different clusters of prehistoric artifacts, indicating that an archaeological site covered much of the bluff. Unfortunately, none of the

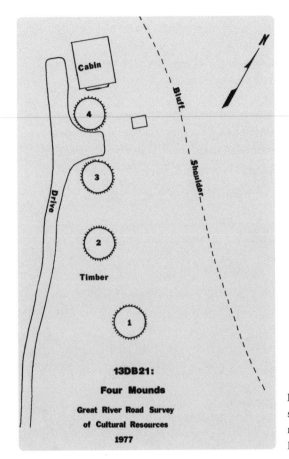

Plat map of Four Mounds
site and nearby structures as
mapped for the Iowa Great
River Roads Survey, 1977.

prehistoric artifacts could be clearly linked to a time period, meaning we do not know how old the sites are. When Anton Till visited the site in 1977, he noted that someone had found a red stone pipe near the mounds. This was probably a catlinite pipe, which was common in the Late Prehistoric period but can also occur in Late Woodland period sites.

✳ TO VISIT

Four Mounds Inn & Conference Center is located at 4900 Peru Road in Dubuque (563-556-1908), www.fourmounds.org.

✳ WANT TO LEARN MORE?

Cechota, Cynthia
1991   To Build the Four Mounds Dream. *Iowa Natural Heritage* (Winter):
        11–13.

Gregory, Michael M.
2008   Phase I Archeological Investigation of the Four Mounds Estate Historic
        District in Dubuque County, Iowa. Reports of Investigations No. 682.
        Great Lakes Archaeological Research Center, Milwaukee.

56 Mines of Spain

✳ Dubuque, Dubuque County

✳ Archaic–Historic

✳ SITE NUMBER 13DB43

THE AREA JUST SOUTH of Dubuque contains the densest concentration of archaeological sites in Iowa. In a 3-mile stretch along the Mississippi, there are more than 250 recorded archaeological sites. Years ago, when the OSA recorded site locations on U.S. Geological Survey maps, this portion of the map had to be photographically enlarged to contain all the sites; otherwise the ink from the site boundaries blurred together.

This region, called the Mines of Spain, is best known as Julien Dubuque's estate, a large area of land that he governed from the 1780s and that was officially deeded to him by the Spanish government in 1796. He lived on the property until his death in 1810. Archaeologists flocked to this area because of the wide range of sites, including those related to Julien Dubuque, numerous mounds, prehistoric camps, rockshelters, historic Indian villages, lead mining sites, and early settler sites.

Sites in the Mines of Spain include Archaic and Woodland occupations, and numerous Woodland mounds, but the area is best known for its protohistoric and early historic occupations. The Meskwaki occupied this area and established a large village, probably in the 1770s. Dubuque, who was among the first Europeans to settle in what is now Iowa, got along well with the Meskwaki, who gave him permission to live and mine lead in the area. He employed the Meskwaki and served as their financial intermediary, converting lead into trade goods through his connections in St. Louis. Archaeologists found numerous lead mining sites in the area, many probably dug by the Meskwaki, others developed later by settlers. People mined lead in the region through the Civil War. Surveyors also found evidence of several lead smelter furnaces, some of which may date to Dubuque's time.

Archaeologists have long tried to find the site of the Meskwaki village near the mouth of Catfish Creek, but with only ambiguous results. Many of the artifacts recovered from this area likely date to the late 18th or early 19th

Julien Dubuque's monument, Mines of Spain State Park, 2007, Dubuque, Dubuque County.

Mines of Spain State Park, 2007, Dubuque, Dubuque County.

century, but researchers have not found any clear evidence of structures or other village features. The Meskwaki buried Dubuque in a log cabin tomb, a traditional manner of burial for their leaders, on the high bluff overlooking Catfish Creek. George Catlin painted this grave in 1835, but by the end of the 19th century it was dilapidated. In 1897, local residents built an imposing stone tower on the bluff to mark the gravesite. The Mines of Spain region is listed as a National Historic Landmark and a state preserve.

☀ TO VISIT

Much of this region is now part of the Mines of Spain Recreation Area, which runs the E. B. Lyons Interpretive Center, 8991 Bellevue Heights, Dubuque, near the intersection of U.S. Highways 52 and 61. It is open Monday–Friday year-round, and on weekends April–October (563-556-0620). Dubuque's grave, as well as several Indian mounds and markers, can be seen at the bluff overlooking the Mississippi, at the end of Monument Drive. The route is not straightforward, but there are signs to the monument, and you can get directions at the interpretive center.

☀ WANT TO LEARN MORE?

Prior, Jean C., Shirley J. Schermer, John Pearson, and Martha A. Maxon
1991   *Natural and Cultural History of the Mines of Spain, Dubuque County, Iowa.* Guidebook 53. Geological Society of Iowa, Iowa City.

Schermer, Shirley J.
2008   The Archaeology of the Mines of Spain: The Meskwaki and Julien Dubuque. *Wisconsin Archeologist* 89:132–149.

Stubbs, Donna L.
2004   Prehistoric Lead Mining in the Dubuque Area. *Journal of the Iowa Archeological Society* 51:9–16.

57 Oneida Cheese Factory
at Bowen's Prairie

✳ *Bowen's Prairie Townsite, Jones County*

✳ *Historic (1873–1904)*

✳ SITE NUMBER 13JN168

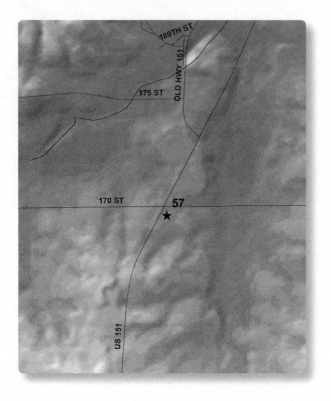

THE STORY OF EARLY settlement and dairying in Jones County blends the research of historians, architects, and archaeologists. The widening of U.S. Highway 151 through northeastern Iowa from two to four lanes in the early 2000s led the OSA to conduct extensive archaeological investigations for the Iowa Department of Transportation. U.S. Highway 151 was originally the Old Military Road, a key transportation corridor linking Dubuque to the Iowa territorial capital at Iowa City. There were several important 19th-century sites along the route, including an 1830s farmstead, the townsite of Bowen's Prairie, and the Oneida Cheese Factory, among the first in the state and the only such enterprise to receive extensive archaeological excavation. Ultimately, all of these sites were incorporated into the Bowen's Prairie Historic Archaeological District.

Once the U.S. government opened the Iowa Territory in 1832, and lured by abundant water, wildlife, timber, building stone, and clay, settlers followed well-worn trails from the Mississippi River across prairies and woodlands to the area between the north and south forks of the Maquoketa River. These pioneers purchased land at $1.25 per acre from the U.S. government, which turned a handy 1,250 percent profit from the sale of territory it had only recently bought from the Meskwaki and Sauk in the Black Hawk Purchase. Very soon, upland prairie farms dotted a 30,000-acre region that became known as "Bowen's Settlement" or "Bowen's Prairie" after Hugh Bowen, the first recorded settler.

For two decades, the area's rich soils supported self-sufficient, family-based farms producing cream, butter, and cheese primarily for home use. By the 1860s, Bowen's Prairie farmers were profiting from the sale of surplus cheese and butter. Commercial dairy production began to replace home production between the late 1860s and the 1870s, with the construction of creameries and cheese factories booming in the late 19th century. By 1873, Bowen's Prairie was home to one of Iowa's three earliest cheese factories.

Alfred Doxsee, an Ohio native, erected the Oneida Cheese Factory in 1873. By the mid-1880s, it, like most other smaller cheese operations, converted to making butter, because it was more profitable than cheese. Between 1893 and 1900, the factory was operated as a cooperative called the Star Creamery.

Below the plowed fields north of the highway, archaeologists uncovered clues that demonstrated the early dairy's transition from making cheese to making butter. In addition to the foundation of the main factory building, they found a well, trash pits, an outhouse pit, and a drainage line connecting a wood-lined trough to a nearby hog lot. During cheese-making, workers dumped the whey into the trough, and it ran down the drain line to provide food for the hogs.

A steam engine, churns, and a milk-cooling chamber found adjacent to a well marked the shift to butter production. Initially, the steam engine

Wooden trough used to transport whey to hog lot as uncovered in excavations at the Oneida Cheese Factory near Bowen's Prairie townsite, facing east, 2001, Jones County.

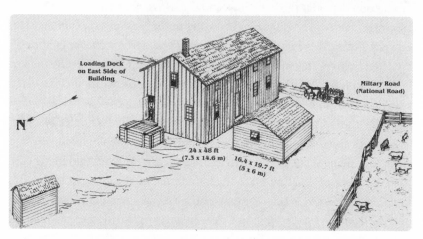

Artist's reconstruction of the Oneida Cheese Factory near Bowen's Prairie townsite, Jones County. Drawing by Angela Collins.

constantly pumped well water into a limestone-lined pool containing "cooley cans" full of milk. The water cooled the milk quickly so that the cream rose faster. Once the factory acquired a mechanical separator in 1893, this pool was no longer needed. Artifacts directly relating to cheese- or butter-making included brass stencil fragments used to mark crates of cheese or butter for shipment, a large milk-strainer, a milk-cooler pail, straight-sided milk cans, stoneware vessels, a glass Babcock milk-test bottle (to test butterfat content), a cream gauge, a thermometer, bucket parts, and a hand-forged metal anchor that probably served as a windmill anchor.

By 1900, the Star Creamery was no longer in business—its equipment was sold, buildings were moved off-site, and land was prepared for use as pasture. Many other small Iowa creameries closed about this time. The mechanization taking place in the butter business, the advent of the railroad for marketing and transporting milk to central creameries, and eventually the spread of the home separator meant that support for numerous small, local creameries no longer existed. The Star Creamery had no direct connection to the railroad, no source of ice except a distant river, and apparently no icehouse—all handicaps for a small operation.

The sites uncovered on Bowen's Prairie provided the first extensive archaeological evidence about northeast Iowa's early Euroamerican settlement and especially the significant role the area played in the foundation of the state's dairy industry. Today, existing dairy farms, creameries, and cheese factories—some reflecting the renewed interest in buying locally produced foods and goods—are a legacy of this past.

✳ TO VISIT

The historic Bowen's Prairie cemetery may still be visited on the south side of U.S. Highway 151 about halfway between the towns of Monticello to the west and Cascade to the east. The area's founding pioneers rest here. The townsite and the footprints of the Oneida Cheese Factory have been destroyed by the highway or are buried beneath the adjoining farm fields.

✳ WANT TO LEARN MORE?

Peterson, Cynthia L., ed.
2006 *Phase III Data Recovery at Five Sites within the Bowen's Prairie Historic Archaeological District, Jones County, Iowa.* Contract Completion Report 1000. Office of the State Archaeologist, University of Iowa, Iowa City.

Peterson, Cynthia L., Clare L. Kernek, and Leah D. Rogers
2005 *Little Dairy on the Prairie: From Butter-makin' Women to High-tech Agriculture.* Office of the State Archaeologist, University of Iowa, Iowa City.

58 Hadfields Cave:
Refuge inside the Cliffs

✳ *Jones County*

✳ *Woodland*

✳ SITE NUMBER 13JN3

BELOW CASCADE, the Maquoketa River hacks its way through the East-Central Iowa Drift Plain, a region of steep rolling hills in the eastern nose of Iowa, cutting across high-relief drainages as it struggles to find the Mississippi River. The river seesaws back and forth across the land, leaving a serpentine channel with sheer bluff walls. The Maquoketa has very little flood plain because the steep valley walls of hard dolomite force it to dig downward, creating an ever-deeper valley, rather than cutting laterally.

As the Maquoketa cuts through bedrock, it exposes a variety of rock types, some soft, others fractured by past geological events. These weaker rocks fall away, leaving voids in the valley walls. Many of them are big enough for people to live in, and archaeologists call them rockshelters (for other examples, see Ginger Stairs [37], Woodpecker Cave [38], and Jackson County rockshelters [59]).

One of these voids is Hadfields Cave, a low-roofed rockshelter a few miles below Cascade excavated by David Benn in the summer of 1972. He originally thought he would be excavating a deep shelter, perhaps one that people occupied over the course of millennia, but the cave turned out to be fairly shallow and contained Late Woodland materials spanning a 500-year period, A.D. 300–800. Benn's crew excavated numerous pits and hearths, and his discoveries helped change our ideas of the Late Woodland. Before this investigation, archaeologists had assumed that people domesticated corn before other crops. However, Benn found more evidence of chenopodium and sunflower crops in the deeper, older levels, while corn appeared to become present in the later occupations of the cave.

Benn's work also brought new insights into ceramic and textile analysis. With the remains he found in Hadfields, he could chart the transition in pot forms from Havana, to Linn, to Madison wares, essentially from

Carved clamshell artifact, Hadfields Cave, Jones County.

the terminal Middle Woodland to the terminal Late Woodland periods. Noting the elaborate cord marks on the shoulders and collars of Madison Ware pots, he was able to show how Indians wove intricate mesh covers for freshly formed clay pots. This mesh burned off when the pot was fired, but it left behind elaborate knotted and woven patterns.

The most celebrated object from Hadfields Cave was a shell gorget, a large segment of shell carved to resemble a spiral rattlesnake with an animal head, perhaps a deer. Benn himself did not uncover this gorget; rather, Boy Scouts who dug in the top few inches of the cave in 1934 discovered it. They were working under the direction of Rev. Albert Coe, a close friend of Charles R. Keyes, a "founding father" of Iowa archaeology (see Weed Park Mounds [62]). Benn later determined that the Boy Scouts probably found the rattlesnake gorget near a pit feature later excavated in 1972 that contained several turtle shell rattles, and may have been part of a cache of ceremonial items deposited during one of the last occupations of the cave. A scout named Robert Brittell kept the gorget as a souvenir, probably without Coe's knowledge. A few years after the excavation, Brittell, then in college, became gravely ill and was expected to die. On his deathbed, he decided to donate the rattlesnake gorget to the state of Iowa for permanent curation. Miraculously, Brittell recovered from his illness, and went on to obtain his Ph.D. and became a dean at the University of Pittsburgh.

☀ TO VISIT

Although Hadfields Cave is on private property, you can visit similar rock-shelters nearby at Whitewater Canyon Wildlife Area. From Cascade, take U.S. Highway 151 east 5 miles to Curoe Road, and head south. The park entrance is 2 miles south; follow the trails to the bottom of the canyon, and you will see many shelters. Brittell's rattlesnake gorget is on permanent display at the Museum of Natural History at the University of Iowa.

☀ WANT TO LEARN MORE?

Benn, David W.
1980 *Hadfields Cave: A Perspective on Late Woodland Culture in Northeastern Iowa*. Report 13. Office of the State Archaeologist, University of Iowa, Iowa City.

Collins, James M.
2000 Some Notes on the Hadfields Cave Rattlesnake Gorget: Part 1, Discovery. *Newsletter of the Iowa Archeological Society* 50(3): 7–9.
2000 Some Notes on the Hadfields Cave Rattlesnake Gorget: Part 2, Bob Brittell's Gift to Iowa. *Newsletter of the Iowa Archeological Society* 50(4): 3–5.

59 Jackson County Rockshelters: Mouse Hollow and Levsen

❉ Jackson County

❉ Archaic–Historic

❉ SITE NUMBER 13JK4

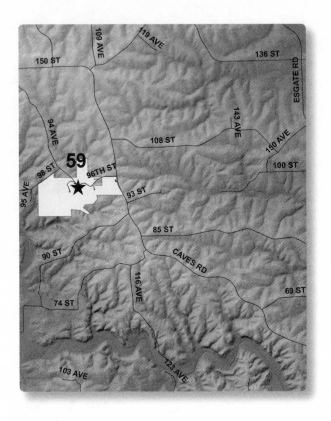

BY EARLY ARCHAIC TIMES, people in eastern Iowa were discovering the benefits of living in rockshelters (see Hadfields Cave [58] and Woodpecker Cave [38]). With the winter sun low on the horizon, south-facing shelter openings proved especially attractive for fall through early spring habitation. Between 1925 and 1936, brothers Paul and Fay Sagers, lifelong residents of Jackson County, amassed one of the largest and most significant archaeological collections from important rockshelter sites in northeastern Iowa.

The Sagers launched their exploration of Jackson and Jones County antiquities while still in their teens, inspired by the discoveries and the large artifact collection of Frank Ellis, a family friend. The impressive rockshelters perched above the Maquoketa River valley in western Jackson County proved irresistible. By the mid-1920s, the Sagers brothers were digging into the deep deposits of sites like the Mouse Hollow and Levsen rockshelters, projects that kept them busy for more than a decade.

The Mouse Hollow rockshelter consists of a long, shallow overhang with a gently sloping floor embedded in the face of a limestone ridge that protrudes into Rodifer Creek southwest of its confluence with the Maquoketa. During the 1920s and 1930s, the Sagers excavated a portion of the shelter's midsection. The numerous stone, pottery, bone, and shell artifacts from the site reveal that people lived here from the Archaic to the historic period — a 6,000-year time span. While Late Woodland pottery predominates, it is the presence of the incised and polished Mississippian ceramics that makes the site renowned to archaeologists. Similar to the Ramey Incised pottery type from the large Mississippian community of Cahokia at East St. Louis, Illinois, this pottery marks Mouse Hollow as one of only a handful of sites in eastern Iowa where Mississippian artifacts have been found.

Fortunately, about the time the Sagers began excavating Mouse Hollow, Paul was introduced to Charles R. Keyes, then director of the Iowa Archaeological Survey (see Weed Park Mounds [62]). Probably at Keyes's request, Paul began keeping a journal of his excavations, making maps, and labeling some of the artifacts he uncovered. Paul and Keyes began a regular correspondence, with Keyes frequently visiting the Sagers's projects, taking his own notes and photographs.

In 1932, Paul began a decades-long exploration of the Levsen rockshelter. The site occupies a high talus slope at the base of a limestone cliff facing the north bank of the Maquoketa River below Canton. The shelter consists of one enormous "room" extending nearly 20 feet into the rock with a vaulted opening 13–20 feet in height and a habitable living area of over 2,000 square feet. The back portion has a 6-feet-high ceiling that was almost completely packed with soil and cultural debris when Paul's excavations began. He

Paul Sagers standing in front of Levsen Rockshelter, Jackson County. Photo courtesy of the State Historical Society of Iowa, Iowa City, Charles R. Keyes Archaeological Collection, and the University of Iowa Office of the State Archaeologist.

Mouse Hollow rockshelter, Jackson County. Photo courtesy of the State Historical Society of Iowa, Iowa City, Charles R. Keyes Archaeological Collection, and the University of Iowa Office of the State Archaeologist.

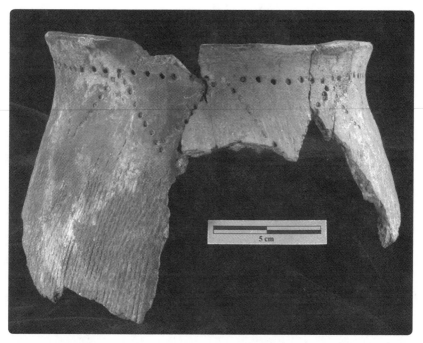

Levsen pottery as found at Levsen rockshelter, Jackson County.

removed and screened nearly all of the deposits in this portion of the shelter, collecting nearly 8,000 artifacts composed of stone, pottery, and bone objects. The stone and pottery artifacts indicate that Levsen, like Mouse Hollow, had a long sequence of occupations, spanning over 6,000 years.

Unlike some collectors who choose to keep their discoveries private, Paul Sagers wanted to share his collection in a location that the public could enjoy. In 1951, he completed a small limestone block structure near the entrance to Maquoketa Caves State Park. He and his wife, Nettie, operated the Sagers Museum for over 30 years. In 1988, six years after Paul's death, the state of Iowa purchased the Sagers Museum. Nettie Sagers gave the archaeological collection as an unrestricted gift to the state. A few years later, OSA cataloged the entire collection, and in 2008, with permission of the Iowa Department of Natural Resources, accepted it for permanent curation. The collection contains nearly 16,000 items from Jackson and Jones County sites, 13 of them rockshelters.

In the 1950s, Wilfred D. Logan, the first archaeologist assigned to Effigy Mounds National Monument, restudied the Mouse Hollow and Levsen collections in tandem with the maps, notes, and drawings made by Sagers and Keyes. Careful examination of these materials allowed Logan to reconstruct the sequence of deposits found in the shelters and determine the associated pottery types. Integrating this information with that from other sites, Logan was able to propose the first detailed outline of Woodland cultures in northeastern Iowa.

Recent radiocarbon analysis of residue removed from a piece of pottery from the Levsen collection as part of a University of Wisconsin–Milwaukee study produced a calendar age of A.D. 165–199. This date nicely matches the late Middle Woodland age of the pottery type — Levsen Punctated — as Logan proposed. It is certain that the Sagers Collection will continue to contribute significant new knowledge about eastern Iowa prehistory well into the future.

✳ TO VISIT

Levsen, Mouse Hollow, and other shelters the Sagers explored are part of today's Maquoketa Caves State Park, 10970 98th Street, Maquoketa (563-652-5833). The former Sagers Museum building has been converted into an interpretive center containing detailed information about the geology of cave formations, park history, and background on the park's early inhabitants. From U.S. Highway 61 north of Maquoketa, head west on Caves Road to 96th Street and the park entrance. The entire Sagers Collection is permanently curated at the OSA, 700 S Clinton Street, Iowa City (319-384-0732). Four large lobby exhibits provide information about the Sagers and their contributions to Iowa archaeology.

✳ WANT TO LEARN MORE?

Chappell, Lauri L.
2011   Paul Sagers: Lasting Impression in Iowa Archaeology. *Newsletter of the Iowa Archeological Society* 61(2): 2–3.

Cordell, John L., and Stephen C. Lensink
2008 Sagers Collection Comes to OSA. *Newsletter of the Iowa Archeological Society* 58(3): 8–9.

Cordell, John L., William Green, and Derrick J. Marcucci
1993 The Paul Sagers Archaeological Collection. In *An Introduction to the Prehistory and History of Maquoketa, Jackson County, Iowa*, ed. Derrick J. Marcucci, Susan L. Gade, Juliet E. Morrow, and Toby A. Morrow, 85–100. Cedar Rapids, Iowa: Cultural Resource Group, Louis Berger and Associates.

Doershuk, John F., and John L. Cordell
2009 Levsen Rockshelter Gets a New AMS Date. *Newsletter of the Iowa Archeological Society* 59(1): 3.

Green, William, Chérie E. Haury, and John L. Cordell
1992 Documenting Southwestern Iowa Prehistory through the Paul Sagers Collection. *Journal of the Iowa Archeological Society* 39:1–14.

Logan, Wilfred D.
1976 *Woodland Complexes in Northeastern Iowa.* Publications in Archeology 15. National Park Service, U.S. Department of the Interior, Washington, D.C.

60 Hurstville Lime Kilns

✳ *Maquoketa, Jones County*

✳ Historic (1870–1930)

✳ SITE NUMBER 13JK191

THE HURSTVILLE Lime Kilns tell a story about both a distinctive geology and a distinctive moment in Iowa's past. The Silurian dolomite of northeast Iowa is known for its beauty and purity. The quarries at Stone City famously provided Anamosa Limestone, a hard, buff-colored banded dolomitic limestone used in architecture and landscaping across eastern Iowa. Unlike regular limestone, which tended to crumble after long exposure to the elements, Anamosa Limestone remained solid. The dolomitic limestone of the area also made excellent quicklime, a necessary ingredient in brick mortar and early cement. This quicklime was pure white and highly adhesive to sand.

Making mortar requires heating limestone in kilns to 825° C (1,500° F) to break down its calcium carbonate into calcium oxide, called quicklime, a caustic powder that irritates the skin and eyes. Before ready sources of coal and gas were available, enormous amounts of wood were burned to make quicklime.

The area around Maquoketa was known for its limestone cliffs, a readily accessible source of the high-quality Silurian dolomitic limestone. In 1870, Alfred Hurst began a small lime kiln, and within a few years he had four large ones running, worked by dozens of men. Teams of men chopped wood on the 3,000 acres of woodlots Hurst owned to burn in the kilns. Horses hauled wagons full of limestone from nearby quarries across the river and walked up a long wooden ramp, from which the stone was dumped into the kilns. Workers hurriedly barreled the quicklime before it reacted with air and lost its potency. A camp named Hurstville where the workers lived grew up next to the kilns.

Hurst died in 1915, and new technologies began to replace the old lime kilns. Newer mortar used hydrated lime, made by a different process. Instead of cooking one batch at a time, manufacturers ran kilns like assembly

Hurstville Lime Kilns, Jackson County.

Workmen's residence, Hurstville Lime Kilns, Jackson County.

lines. After Hurst's kilns were shut down in 1930, they and Hurstville were left to decay. Soon all that was left of the site were the kilns, and they, too, started to crumble.

Alarmed by the possible loss of Maquoketa's history, Paul Sagers (see Jackson County Rockshelters [59]) and Ed Kirchhoff led a campaign to have the kilns restored, beginning in the 1970s. By 1985, community support led to the stabilization of the kilns. Now open to the public as a small park, the site is owned by the Jackson County Historical Society and is managed by the Jackson County Conservation Board.

✳ TO VISIT

The kilns are located on U.S. Highway 61, 2 miles north of Maquoketa. The Hurstville camp, where the workers lived, is located in the auto salvage yard to the east.

✳ WANT TO LEARN MORE?

Radsal, Dave
n.d.   *Kilns That Built the Midwest Fire Up Again to Boil Corn.* Brochure.
       www.mycountyparks.com/county/Jackson/Park/Hurstville-Lime
       -Kilns.aspx.

Rogers, Leah D.
1994   *Historic Archaeological Resources of the Maquoketa Locality, Jackson
       County, Iowa: Phase I Archaeological Survey.* Mount Vernon, Iowa:
       Leah D. Rogers.

61 Antoine LeClaire House

* Davenport, Scott County
* Historic (1853)
* SITE NUMBER 13ST184

IT SEEMS LIKE Antoine LeClaire tried to build Iowa single-handedly. He founded its first large town, Davenport. He built the first commercial ferry across the Mississippi, the first planned hotel in Iowa, and the first foundry in Davenport. He helped found the first bank in Iowa, and served as the first justice of the peace and postmaster in Iowa.

LeClaire was a close associate of just about every important midwesterner in the early 19th century. His mentor was William Clark, of Lewis and Clark fame. LeClaire translated Black Hawk's autobiography. He helped his good friend Colonel George Davenport financially, and named the largest town in the Iowa Territory for him. He befriended the chiefs of every tribe in the region—Sauk, Osage, Kansa, Ojibwa, and Ho-Chunk (Winnebago)—and translated for them at treaty negotiations, where he befriended U.S. generals and politicians.

LeClaire straddled the European and Indian worlds easily. Born in 1797 in what is now Michigan, he was Métis, the son of a French Canadian trader father and a Potawatomi mother. Growing up at his father's trading post, he learned numerous Native American languages and became familiar with the complex social and political systems of tribes in the Midwest. His father sided with the Americans during the War of 1812, and when he was captured and held by the British, William Clark cared for the young Antoine. Clark had him educated in St. Louis and steered his career into government service, where he used his language and cultural skills to negotiate with tribes. From his headquarters at Fort Armstrong in Rock Island, he became lifelong friends with Colonel George Davenport. LeClaire's marriage in 1820 to Marguerite LaPage, the daughter of a French trader and Sauk leader, integrated him into that powerful tribe.

After the failed Black Hawk uprising of 1832, in which Black Hawk led the Sauk on a suicidal campaign against white settlements that ended with the tribe's decimation, LeClaire was the only one that all parties trusted as a translator for the subsequent treaty. He also wrote down and translated Black Hawk's famous autobiography, considered to be one of the greatest American historical texts. For his treaty work he was rewarded with large grants of land in Iowa from the Sauk and Potawatomi; these lands included the future locations of Moline, LeClaire, and Davenport, which soon became the largest town in prestatehood Iowa. His era as a translator and negotiator ending with all tribes being shifted out of the region, LeClaire turned his attention toward developing the Iowa Territory and Davenport. He made a fortune in land sales and through businesses he founded in the early days of settlement.

In 1853, LeClaire began work on a grand mansion on the bluffs above Davenport; this Italianate house was one of the earliest great residences in Iowa. He lived there until his death in 1861, and his family continued to reside in it until 1881. The Roman Catholic Diocese of Davenport purchased the house as a home for its bishop; it was used for this purpose until 1906. After this period, the house became a boardinghouse. Alarmed at the house's deterioration, the city of Davenport purchased it in 1976, and it has been under intermittent renovation since then.

In 2002, archaeologists excavated under the porches at the LeClaire House prior to a renovation project. The top of a well and cistern, a large brick-lined tank used to store rainwater collected from the roof, emerged in a trench. Wells and cisterns are often archaeological jackpots because they can contain layered deposits of artifacts, with the oldest artifacts at the bottom and the more recent at the top. The bottom of the well and cistern probably contained artifacts from the LeClaire occupation. However, full excavation would have been expensive and destructive, and it was not necessary for the renovation to proceed. After careful consideration, archaeologists and renovators decided that the well and cistern should be left in place for future researchers.

※ TO VISIT

The LeClaire House is located at 630 E 7th Street, Davenport. The house is maintained by the Scott County Historic Preservation Society. It is open only sporadically for tours; check the *Quad Cities Times* (qctimes.com) for tour dates. The grounds are open to the public.

✳ WANT TO LEARN MORE?

Annals of Iowa

1863   Memoir of Antoine Le Claire, Esquire, of Davenport, Iowa. *Annals of Iowa* 1/2:144–149.

Schoen, Christopher M.

2003   *Archaeological Monitoring at Site 13ST184, the Antoine LeClaire House in Davenport, Scott County, Iowa.* Marion, Iowa: Louis Berger & Associates, Louis Berger Group.

Snyder, Charles

1941   Antoine Leclaire, the First Proprietor of Davenport. *Annals of Iowa* 23:79–117.

62 Weed Park Mounds: "Forever Undisturbed"

 * *Muscatine County*
 * *Woodland*
 * SITE NUMBER 13MC43

ON MAY 29, 1946, below the bright blue skies over Muscatine's Weed Park, and standing on the tallest of 14 prehistoric earthen mounds, Charles R. Keyes, one of Iowa archaeology's "founding fathers," addressed a crowd of civic leaders, Kiwanis Club officials, dignitaries from the State Historical Society of Iowa and the Putnam Museum, and local citizens. Boy Scouts stood sentry atop the other mounds, and the Muscatine High School band opened and closed the event with two rousing marches. The celebration marked the dedication of the mounds and the placement of a large commemorative granite and brass marker. In his short speech, Keyes noted, "We have a fine group of Indian mounds here, one of the finest remaining in the state of Iowa," adding his hope that they might "remain forever undisturbed."

Thousands of mounds and earthworks once existed throughout the Mississippi valley, and pioneer Iowans' fascination with them mirrored that of the rest of the country. Inquisitive settlers began digging into mounds almost before they had unpacked their wagons. Within a few decades, local scientific societies such as the Davenport Academy of Natural Sciences (DANS) and the Muscatine Academy of Sciences (MAS) took over, dismantling and leveling dozens of mounds from Bellevue to Burlington. Excavations at sites such as Cook Farm in Scott County, Toolesboro in Louisa County (65), and Pine Creek and Weed Park in Muscatine County were undertaken to obtain relics and human skeletons. Artifacts not retained in private hands became the nucleus of many local and regional museum collections and were traded to other institutions throughout the eastern United States.

In 1879, Theron Thompson, a member of the MAS, reported to the Smithsonian Institution on groups of mounds and earthworks throughout

Charles R. Keyes, 1920s.
Photo courtesy of Cornell
College, Mount Vernon.

Muscatine County. He estimated these mounds ranged in size from 3 to 30 feet in diameter and from 6 inches to 5 feet in height. In Weed Park alone, he trenched and leveled half of a group of 20, finding only charcoal and bits of mussel shell. Elsewhere his efforts were more fruitful, producing human bones and some artifacts.

Until the late 1800s, efforts by Thompson and others were generally directed at determining the origin of the mounds. The early idea that they were created by a race of "Moundbuilders," not American Indians, had, by the turn of the century, been jettisoned by most (see Malchow Mounds [66]). Although the DANS and the Bureau of American Ethnology excavated the Pine Creek mounds south of Wildcat Den as late as 1914, from the 1920s to 1950s systematic study of most Iowa mounds fell largely within the purview of Charles R. Keyes and his remarkable assistant, Ellison Orr.

Above: Commemorative plaque, Weed Park Mounds, Muscatine County.

Right: Aerial view, Weed Park Mounds outlined in white, Muscatine County. Courtesy of George A. Horton, photographer.

As director of the Archaeological Survey for the State Historical Society of Iowa between 1921 and 1951, Keyes, a professor of German language and literature at Cornell College, and Orr, a renaissance man of many talents including survey, investigated and documented artifact collections and sites throughout the state. Such efforts established the basic framework for understanding Iowa prehistory. Their 1930s reconnaissance survey of mound groups provided maps and plans for many Mississippi River bluff-top sites in Iowa along with recommendations for their preservation and purchase by the state. By this time, there was good reason. Thousands of mounds that once existed were gone—plowed under, built over, and looted.

The 1946 dedication of the Weed Park Mounds was a fitting coda to the lifetime endeavors of Keyes and Orr. Effigy Mounds National Monument near McGregor, dedicated three years later, also owed its creation to their sustained efforts and lobbying.

The 1976 passage of Iowa's protective burial legislation (see Old Pacific City Cemetery [14]) eventually put mound groups off-limits to any type of invasive study. Field investigations since that time are confined to survey, mapping, and types of nondestructive geophysical survey. Such investigations at Weed Park in the 1970s demonstrated that the mound group there is actually larger than city leaders thought in 1946. Today, we know that 15 conical, three elongated-conical, and three linear mounds are present; the largest, adjacent to the bluff edge, stands 6 feet in height and 40 feet in diameter. Eight smaller mounds, 2 to 4 feet in height, extend in a line to the southwest. Based on research elsewhere, we know that people throughout the Woodland period reused this site predominantly as a cemetery for more than 1,000 years.

✸ TO VISIT

The Weed Park Mounds are located in Muscatine. From U.S. Highway 61, follow Colorado Street a short distance to signs for Weed Park. Mounds occur in the south park unit. Cars can be parked alongside the road within easy walking distance to the mounds.

✳ WANT TO LEARN MORE?

1946   Audio Recording of May 29, 1946, radio broadcast at Weed Park.
        Courtesy University of Iowa Library.

Alex, Lynn M.

2009   Orr, Ellison James. In *The Biographical Dictionary of Iowa*, ed. David
        Hudson, Marvin Bergman, and Loren Horton, 390–392. Iowa City:
        University of Iowa Press.

Perry, Michael

2009   Keyes, Charles Reuben. In *The Biographical Dictionary of Iowa*, ed.
        David Hudson, Marvin Bergman, and Loren Horton, 282–284.
        Iowa City: University of Iowa Press.

Thompson, Theron

1879   Burial Mounds in the Mississippi Valley. *American Antiquarian* 2:60.

1880   Mounds in Muscatine County, Iowa, and Rock Island County,
        Illinois. In *Annual Report of the Board of Regents of the Smithsonian
        Institution, Showing the Operations, Expenditures, and Condition of
        the Institution for the Year 1879*, 359–363. Washington, D.C.: U.S.
        Government Printing Office.

63 Ancient Village Life at McNeal Fan

※ *Muscatine County*

※ *Archaic and Woodland*

※ SITE NUMBER 13MC15

ARCHAEOLOGISTS NORMALLY associate village sites containing many houses with the Late Prehistoric or Woodland period, when farming supported larger settlements. But the roots of the prehistoric village go back much farther in Iowa. The McNeal Fan site southwest of Muscatine, dating to the end of the Middle Archaic period, about 4,800 years ago, arguably has the oldest village in Iowa. Older locations, such as the Palace site of 6,800 years ago (24), have evidence of substantial houses, but these houses were probably occupied sequentially, not all at the same time, so they could not be considered villages.

Southwest of Muscatine is a large curve in the Mississippi River valley, where the floodplain widens out, creating a broad expanse covering more than 40 square miles. This was historically called Muscatine Island or Muscatine Slough, although it is technically neither an island nor a slough. In his 1903 *History of Iowa*, Benjamin Gue mapped hundreds of mounds on the bluffs that curve around the floodplain like an amphitheater; most of these mounds have since been destroyed. Keokuk Lake, covering about 10 acres, lies near the center of Muscatine Slough, a drained vestige of a much larger lake that once covered more than 2 square miles. Near the former Keokuk Lake, and along the terraces at the base of the bluffs, is a remarkable series of sites called Eisele's Hill, which were excavated prior to an expansion of U.S. Highway 61 beginning in the 1990s.

One of those sites is the McNeal Fan site. Archaeologists from Bear Creek Archaeology excavated possible houses here that date from the end of the Middle Archaic and the Early Woodland periods. Exposing large blocks of the site, measuring hundreds of square yards, they found two circular houses dating to the late Early Woodland period, about 2,200 years ago. Found in association with the houses were pottery, points, fire-cracked rock, cobble tools, flaking debris, and about 70 features including pits and fireplaces.

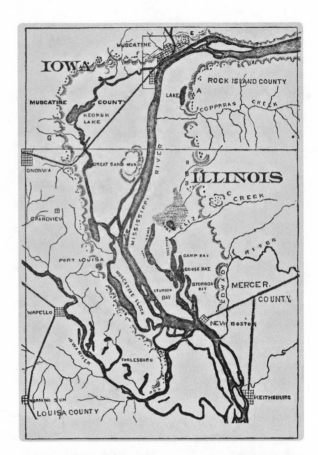

Benjamin Gue's map showing Muscatine Slough and Keokuk Lake. From Gue's *History of Iowa* (1903).

A Keokuk ax from Iowa County similar to those found at an Eisele's Hill site, Muscatine County. Photo courtesy of the State Historical Society of Iowa, Iowa City, Charles R. Keyes Archaeological Collection, and the University of Iowa Office of the State Archaeologist.

At deeper levels, more than 6 feet below the surface, the site contained a late Middle Archaic occupation; this layer was about a foot thick, had darker soils, and contained more than 10,000 artifacts. These included T-drills, Osceola-type spear points, grooved "Keokuk" axes, fire-cracked rock, flaking debris, and cobble tools. This layer dated to approximately 4,800 years ago, and within it researchers found evidence of as many as eight houses. They were shallow oval basins, roughly 20 × 33 feet, with a central post.

Although not the oldest houses excavated in Iowa, those at the McNeal Fan site reveal the earliest evidence of village planning. Some of the houses overlapped, but most were centered around what archaeologists called a "commons area." Within this central plaza were numerous features, including communal roasting pits. Radiocarbon dates suggest people visited or reoccupied this site several times over more than a century. The generations-long use of the site resulted in a thick layer of darker soil, stained by charcoal from fires and decayed organic material.

Although there was no evidence of domestic crops at the Middle Archaic occupation of McNeal Fan, within a few centuries people at other Iowa sites were cultivating crops. Perhaps the McNeal Fan occupants were utilizing domesticated plants, but in a way that is not recognizable, or perhaps the amalgamation of houses into villages in Iowa predates the appearance of farming.

✳ TO VISIT

From Muscatine, head southwest on U.S. Highway 61; drive past the airport. The McNeal Fan site is located deep underground below the highway on the terrace just before you drive up the bluffs.

✳ WANT TO LEARN MORE?

Benn, David W., ed.

2006 *Phase III Archeological Data Recovery from the McNeal Fan (13MC15), Eisele's Hill Locality, Muscatine County, Iowa*. BCA #629. Bear Creek Archeology, Cresco, Iowa.

Benn, David W., and Joe B. Thompson

1999 Recent Excavations at the Eisele's Hill Locality, Muscatine County. *Newsletter of the Iowa Archeological Society* 49(1): 4–5, 49(2): 4–5.

64 McKinney Site: Does "X" Mark the Site?

✳ *Louisa County*

✳ *Late Prehistoric–Protohistoric*

✳ SITE NUMBER 13LA1

HISTORICAL CONCLUSIONS are not always hard and fast. A brass plaque installed during a ceremony in 1973 near the Toolesboro Mounds National Historic Landmark (65) commemorated the spot where, 300 years earlier, Father Jacques Marquette and explorer Louis Joliet were thought to have first set foot on Iowa soil—the earliest known Europeans to have done so. Marquette's journal described the landfall spot as a short distance up a major western tributary of the Mississippi where the party encountered three villages within about 1.5 miles of one another. One "peouarea" village consisted of about 300 lodges. The Peouarea were an Algonquian-speaking Illini (Illinois) people. Even by the time of Marquette's visit, the villagers already owned guns and other French trade goods.

On an upland divide above the Iowa River a short distance from its juncture with the Mississippi, and adjacent to today's Toolesboro Mounds National Historic Landmark, John B. Newhall in 1841 first reported an earthen enclosure or "old fort." Newhall described finding abundant pieces of pottery decorated with geometric designs and sporting wide handles. While professional archaeologists confirmed the presence of the 2,000-year-old Middle Woodland burial mounds that make up the Toolesboro Mounds National Historic Landmark at this location, they also detected evidence for a sizable Late Prehistoric Oneota Indian village of a later time period. The ceramics Newhall found fit well with this new site, named the McKinney site after the landowner. Was this the remnants of the Peouarea settlement Marquette and Joliet visited? Its location certainly seemed to correspond with the map attributed to Marquette, and one archaeologist reported finding Euroamerican trade goods at the site.

Oneota is a Late Prehistoric (A.D. 1100) to early historic (A.D. 1700) cultural tradition of the upper Midwest with sites stretching from the Great Lakes to the eastern Great Plains, including dozens in Iowa (see Blood Run [2], Upper Iowa Enclosures [43], and the Dixon site [10]). Archaeologists generally agree that Chiwere Siouan–speaking peoples, including the Ioway, Otoe, Ho-Chunk (Winnebago), and Missouria, descended from people of the Oneota tradition. The Omaha, Ponca, Kansa, and Osage, Dhegihan Siouan speakers, may have as well. Tracing people's ancestry into the dim reaches of prehistoric time is tricky.

Researchers know that early French traders and explorers did visit Ioway Indian villages on the Upper Iowa River and learned that similar villages in the Iowa Great Lakes region were populated by people such as the Ioway, Otoe, and Omaha. Archaeology at these sites reveals Native-made artifacts (particularly pottery tempered with shell, having wide handles and broad, geometric designs) alongside early French trade items, large rectangular houses, hundreds of storage pits, and other lifeway patterns that have come to be recognized as characteristic of Oneota.

French trade ring (sometimes called Jesuit rings), 17th century, found at the Iliniwek village site, Clark County, Missouri. Courtesy of Roger Boyd, photographer.

Artifacts from the McKinney site environs demonstrate that many people throughout prehistory utilized the area, including the Oneota. In addition to unrecorded collecting and looting since the late 1800s, weekend excavations were undertaken at the McKinney site by John H. Bailey, director of the Putnam Museum and the Quad Cities Archaeological Society in 1946 and 1947. OSA archaeologist Joseph A. Tiffany and Richard G. Slattery, from the Iowa Archeological Society, carried out a series of field school excavations at the site in the 1970s and early 1980s. They were followed by Eric Hollinger, from the University of Illinois, in the mid-1990s.

The archaeologists found hearths and more than 100 overlapping, subsurface storage pits of several shapes and sizes. Many of the pits had clay caps, probably to seal their contents, similar to the Dixon site (10). These would have included dried produce from Oneota gardens, perhaps jerked meat from the hunt, and household valuables. Surprisingly, indigenous plants like erect knotweed and little barley were still being grown alongside corn, beans, and squash. Bones of deer, beaver, turtle, and fish were in abundance, but there were very few bison bones.

Post molds at the site (the footprint of former structural posts) suggested large houses, although their exact shape and size were not determined. The archaeologists recovered thousands of artifacts (over 50,000 from the mid-1990s alone), including Oneota pottery — much of it tempered with burned and ground shell temper, having broad-trailed geometric decorations and wide handles. Other characteristic Oneota items included chipped stone scrapers and arrow points, pipes and pieces of red pipestone (see Blood Run [2]), and a small hematite tablet bearing the image of a hawkman or thunderbird. They found no French trade goods or other evidence of Euroamerican contact. The site, which measures close to 40 acres, had probably been reused by Oneota people over a period of time, but was apparently vacated before the 1600s.

In the meantime, scholars scrutinizing the original descriptions and maps attributed to Father Marquette detected some ambiguity, suggesting that the French party encountered the Illini villages closer to the mouth of the Des Moines River rather than the Iowa. In the mid-1980s, archaeologists reported the discovery of a large site in Clark County, northeast Missouri, not far from the confluence of the Mississippi with the Des Moines. Excavations at this Iliniwek Village State Historic site have revealed long rectangular houses, a type of Native-made pottery called Danner Ware, and French trade goods, including some distinctive rings of the late 17th century. Danner Ware is typically associated with Illini groups, including the Peouarea.

Disappointingly for the people of southeastern Iowa, the inhabitants at McKinney may have moved away shortly before Marquette and Joliet paddled by. The French duo likely stopped near the mouth of the Des Moines at the Iliniwek site. The location of this settlement as described by Marquette, the presence of pottery known to have been made by the very Illini people named by Marquette, and the type of datable French trade goods found here align very well with the description and timing of the 1673 visit.

Intriguingly, a small amount of pottery from Iliniwek is Oneota. Neutron activation study, which determines the chemical composition of the pottery clay, indicates that the Oneota pottery found at Iliniwek derived from both local and nonlocal clays. Does this suggest that a small number of Chiwere Siouan–speaking people were actually living at Iliniwek, and if so, why, and where did they come from?

The McKinney site still has much to reveal. Was the earthen enclosure, or "old fort," built by people living at the McKinney village, or is the earthwork Middle Woodland in age and associated with the nearby Middle Woodland burial mounds? Did the Oneota people move away just as Europeans were about to arrive? Had they been frightened off by the presence of Illini peoples less than 100 miles away? Could some of them have been living at Iliniwek? Only additional research may provide answers.

✳ TO VISIT

The McKinney site is near the Toolesboro Mounds National Historic Landmark (65). Take Highway 99 to Toolesboro. Although the site is on private property, exhibits in the small interpretive center at Toolesboro include information on the McKinney site. See www.iowahistory.org/historic-sites /toolesboro-mounds.

The Iliniwek Village State Historic site is near Wayland, Missouri, about 80 miles south of the Toolesboro Mounds National Historic Landmark: http://mostateparks.com/park/iliniwek-village-state-historic-site.

✳ WANT TO LEARN MORE?

Grantham, Larry D.

1993   The Illini Village of the Marquette and Jolliet Voyage of 1673. *Missouri Archaeologist* 54:1–20.

Hollinger, R. Eric

2005   *Conflict and Culture Change in the Late Prehistoric and Early Historic American Midcontinent.* Ph.D. diss., University of Illinois, Urbana-Champaign. Ann Arbor, MI: University Microfilms.

Slattery, Richard G., George A. Horton, and Michael E. Ruppert

1975   The McKinney Village Site: An Oneota Site in Southeastern Iowa. *Journal of the Iowa Archeological Society* 22:35–61.

Tiffany, Joseph A.

1988   Preliminary Report on Excavations at the McKinney Oneota Village Site (13LA1), Louisa County, Iowa. *Wisconsin Archeologist* 69:227–312.

65 Toolesboro Mounds National Historic Landmark

* Toolesboro, Louisa County
* Woodland
* SITE NUMBER 13LA29

IN 1841, John B. Newhall published the earliest reference to the earthen mounds and adjoining octagonal earthwork north of the town of Blackhawk (later Toolesboro) in *Sketches of Iowa or the Emigrants Guide*. An East-Coaster, Newhall emigrated in the early 1830s to what was then the Black Hawk Purchase to settle and promote his adopted homeland. He turned out to be a pretty good "spin doctor." Settlers came, built farms, and created towns. Not long after the publication of his guide, the mounds he described above the Iowa River near its confluence with the Mississippi (and dozens of others) were dug into by curious landowners or used as the base and cellars for new farmhouses. The original 6-feet-high walls of the earthwork or "old fort" Newhall reported were virtually plowed away (see McKinney site [64]).

From the outset, locals recognized the Toolesboro Mounds, estimated as averaging from 20 to 30 feet in height and about 80 feet in circumference, as burial sites. The skeletal remains and accompanying artifacts within and beneath were touted as some of the finest "relics" ever found. It was not long before such discoveries came to the attention of budding scientific academies, whose own archaeological endeavors centered on these highly visible and often richly furnished sepulchers with the goal of amassing collections for public edification. The Davenport Academy of Natural Sciences (DANS), founded in 1867, led the way in eastern Iowa, exploring mounds along both sides of the Mississippi.

A series of weekend and summertime "digs" by the DANS, the Muscatine Academy of Sciences, and local "explorers" meant that by 1886, most if not all of the 12–14 mounds originally recorded at Toolesboro had been opened, and some completely dismantled. People had also dug into a second group of as many as eight mounds about a half mile southeast of Toolesboro. The

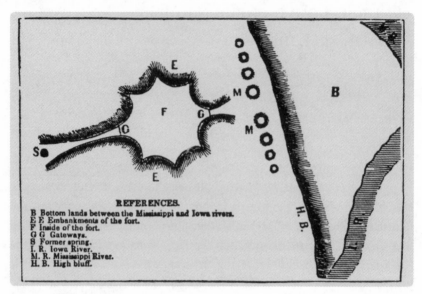

John B. Newhall's 1841 map of earthworks and mounds at the McKinney and Toolesboro sites, Louisa County. Original from *Sketches of Iowa, or the Emigrant's Guide* (1841).

discovery of exquisite stone pipes carved into the forms of birds and mammals, hammered copper celts and pins wrapped in woven cloth, freshwater pearl jewelry, mica mirrors, worked chunks of obsidian, finely decorated pottery vessels, and large whelk shells rewarded these efforts.

Although the DANS's own *Proceedings* published some details of mound construction, including descriptions and drawings of burials, and reported the results of artifact and skeletal analyses, excavation records were minimal. Academy members, while "intelligently interested" in science, were not actual scientists. Many were advocates of the mound-builder myth (see Malchow Mounds [66]), which denied Indian authorship of these ancient monuments. It would be decades before anyone attempted to apply new standards of survey and study to the Toolesboro Mounds and their contents. No others were excavated.

Nineteenth-century property records and the DANS's own documents suggest that only seven of the original mounds at Toolesboro make up the current National Historic Landmark. Archaeologists identify these mounds as mortuary structures belonging to the Havana tradition (ca. 200 B.C.–

A.D. 300), one of several regional traditions that existed throughout eastern North America during the Middle Woodland period. People of the Havana tradition participated in a vast exchange network that archaeologists call Hopewell. The copper, obsidian, mica, and marine shell artifacts found in the mounds had non-Iowa origins, and their style and workmanship reflect an artistry and craft shared among groups of interacting Havana-Hopewell societies 2,000 years ago.

We know about the Middle Woodland people who built the Toolesboro Mounds exclusively from their cemetery. No associated village has ever been found. The location of the mounds within easy access to two major rivers and the presence of significant quantities of Hopewell materials suggest that the area may have served as an exchange center among Middle Woodland societies. But did it? Imagine if what we surmised about modern Davenport or Sioux City derived only from inferences we made from the wealthier graves in the city cemeteries.

State law now protects the Toolesboro Mounds from any kind of disturbance, scientific or otherwise. Current research centers on the rediscovery of the large, geometric-shaped earthwork that archaeologists suspect was an integral part of a sacred Middle Woodland landscape that included the mounds. Aerial photography and the use of lidar topographic imagery reveal tantalizing bumps, shadows, and a horseshoe-shaped feature to the north of the National Historic Monument. These may be remnants of the "old fort" and possibly some of the lost mounds. Nondestructive geophysical study in the near future may reveal some answers (see Kimball [3]).

❋ TO VISIT

The site is on the north edge of Toolesboro along State Highway 99. The 5-acre site includes several large surviving mounds, an education center, and a prairie demonstration plot. The State Historical Society of Iowa owns and preserves the Toolesboro Indian Mounds and Museum. The mounds are listed on the National Register of Historic Places and designated as a National Historic Landmark and a state preserve. See www.iowahistory .org/historic-sites/toolesboro-mounds.

✳ WANT TO LEARN MORE?

Alex, Lynn M., and William Green

1995   *Toolesboro Mounds National Historic Landmark: Archaeological Analysis and Report.* Research Papers 20, no. 4. Office of the State Archaeologist, University of Iowa, Iowa City.

Anderson, Duane C.

1975   The Development of Archaeology in Iowa: An Overview. *Proceedings of the Iowa Academy of Science* 82:71–86.

Herzberg, Ruth, and John Pearson

2001   *The Guide to Iowa's State Preserves.* Iowa City: University of Iowa Press.

Starr, Frederick

1897   The Davenport Academy of Natural Sciences. *Popular Science Monthly* 51:83–97.

Whittaker, William E., and William Green

2010   Early and Middle Woodland Earthwork Enclosures in Iowa. *North American Archaeologist* 31(1): 27–57.

66 Mounds and More Mounds at Malchow

❋ Malchow Mounds State Preserve, Des Moines County

❋ Woodland

❋ SITE NUMBER 13DM4

EARLY SETTLERS WERE astonished by the enormous numbers of mounds found along the Mississippi bluffs in Iowa. To them, it was inconceivable that Indians could have built thousands of earthworks over so much of the continent because they thought Indians were childlike savages incapable of the planning and organization needed to construct so many large and beautiful structures. Settlers compared Indians to bears and wolves, dangerous and unpredictable, creatures that needed to be removed before "true" civilization could take root.

In the 19th century, a convenient lie took root. Many Americans believed Indians were a degraded race that had arrived just a century or so before Europeans, and these savages systematically killed off the older, noble civilization that had constructed mounds and complex earthworks that amazed early European explorers. This lie was seductive. It eliminated any guilt settlers might feel at removing Indians, for they were invaders far worse than Europeans, having completely killed off their antecedents, whereas the American government only killed Indians when they did not cooperate with attempts at civilizing them. Pseudoscience seemed to support the idea that the mound builders were not Indians, but a superior, vanished race. The artifacts and tools found in mounds were not the same as those used by the Indians of the 19th century, and the shape of the ancient skulls looked different from more contemporary ones. Some Indians denied any knowledge of mound building, and settlers used these denials as proof that no Indians had ever built mounds. A charlatan named William Pidgeon even claimed to have interviewed "Dee-Coo-Dah," the last surviving member of the noble mound builders, hiding in Wisconsin, who imparted to Pidgeon the mystical secrets of the mounds.

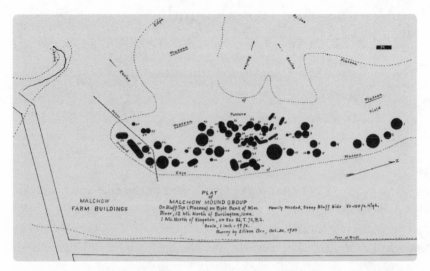

Ellison Orr's 1935 map of the Malchow mound group, Des Moines County. Photo courtesy of the State Historical Society of Iowa, Iowa City, Charles R. Keyes Archaeological Collection, and the University of Iowa Office of the State Archaeologist.

The myth of the mound builders was complete nonsense. There were numerous historical accounts of Indians building mounds, and there were plenty of excavated mounds that showed historical Indians had been building them all along. While older mounds had stone tools and ceramic pots that modern Indians did not use, newer mounds had brass pots and other European trade goods that settlers knew Indians used. The skeletons of modern Indians were very similar to those of the mound builders. Traits seen in mound builders' skulls that were supposedly different from those of modern Indians, such as flattened foreheads, could be seen in living Indians who still practiced older traditions of infant head shaping.

Scientific consensus that Indians built all the mounds did not occur until the 1880s and 1890s, at about the time that Native peoples ceased to be a threat to the United States. It was only when Indians were no longer a danger to settlers that they were given credit for more than 2,000 years of mound building.

One of the largest surviving collections of Indian mounds in Iowa is the Malchow mound group, which includes approximately 60 mounds along

Conical mound, Malchow mound group, 1968, Des Moines County.

the bluff edge north of Kingston. So many mounds are crammed into a small space that it is hard to tell where they begin and end. Charles R. Keyes first described about 30 mounds, and when Ellison Orr mapped the site in 1934, he documented 59 mounds. His was not the last word, though; when the site was digitally remapped in 2009, five more possible mounds became apparent. It was impossible to tell if the mounds along the south bluff edge were built as long linear mounds or if they were smaller round mounds packed together so closely that they now appeared to be linear mounds. The Malchow Mounds became part of the Iowa State Preserve System in 1976.

☀ TO VISIT

The Malchow Mounds are just off County Road 99 north of Kingston, about 15 miles north of Burlington. Look for the sign on the west side of the road. Parking is available; it is a steep climb up the bluff, but worth it.

✳ WANT TO LEARN MORE?

Herzberg, Ruth, and John Pearson
2001   *The Guide to Iowa's State Preserves*. Iowa City: University of Iowa Press.

Orr, Ellison
1935   *Report of a Statewide Reconnaissance Survey of Indian Mound Groups and Excavations of Camp Sites*. Iowa Archaeological Reports 2.

Whittaker, William E.
2010   *Digital Mapping Survey of the Malchow Mound Group (13DM4) Des Moines County, Iowa*. Contract Completion Report 1750. Office of the State Archaeologist, University of Iowa, Iowa City.

67 Is There an Adena or Hopewell Ring Enclosure at the Poisel Mounds?

✳ *Des Moines County*

✳ *Woodland*

✳ SITE NUMBER 13DM226

IN THE EARLY AND MIDDLE Woodland periods, roughly 500 B.C.– A.D. 300, people in the eastern United States constructed large earthworks —linear mounds that extended hundreds of feet, geometric enclosures covering acres of land, ditches that circled large mounds—all part of a cultural system archaeologists today do not understand very well. This Adena and Hopewell tradition of building large earthworks extended to the Mississippi valley, but did not extend much beyond it. Iowa has only five known sites that might include Adena or Hopewell enclosures, all near the Mississippi.

One of these is the Poisel site, a cluster of about nine conical (round) mounds along a bluff overlooking the Mississippi valley. These mounds are not especially noteworthy, except Mound 1, which is large, 90 feet in diameter and 4.5 feet high, and is surrounded by a shallow ring ditch that is 200 feet in diameter on its outside and 140 feet on its inside and is 8–12 inches deep. This ring is not readily visible on the surface. An archaeologist first noticed it in the 1970s, but a decade later a second archaeologist missed it entirely when mapping the site. In 2009, a digital survey of the mound group found the ring again, obscured by grass but made visible during digital mapping (see Litka site [7]).

How old is the Poisel ring? Although the site has not been excavated, habitations nearby contain Early and Middle Woodland materials. Simple mounds with large rings around them are more common at Early Woodland sites than Middle Woodland sites, suggesting Poisel is Early Woodland, but this cannot be confirmed without excavation.

Why would Native Americans build a ring around a mound? It is impossible to be certain about the mindset of people who lived 2,000 years ago,

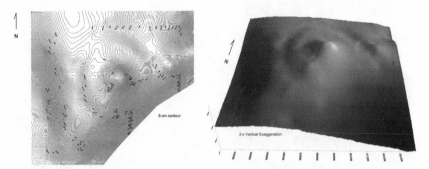

Shaded relief map, Mound #1 with possible enclosure, Poisel mound group, Des Moines County.

Digital survey, 2009, Poisel mound group, Des Moines County.

but using the cosmology of existing Native Americans, we can make reasonable guesses. Some anthropologists who have studied ancient cosmologies, such as Robert L. Hall, view enclosures around graves as a supernatural boundary. Many historical Indians considered circles to be geometric shapes that resisted magic and other supernatural forces. The ring ditch boundary may be intended to protect the grave of an important person from being disturbed by outside magic or, conversely, to contain powerful spirits within the circle. The Turkey River Mounds (54) are possibly examples of the latter.

✳ TO VISIT

The Poisel Mounds are privately owned, and the landowner is, fortunately, fiercely protective of the mounds and does not allow visitors. If you want to get a sense of how the mounds look, the Malchow Mounds (66) are in the same general region of the Mississippi bluffs and are publicly accessible. Likewise, the Turkey River Mounds (54) are accessible and also contain a ring enclosure.

✳ WANT TO LEARN MORE?

Hall, Robert L.

1976   Ghosts, Water Barriers, Corn, and Sacred Enclosures in the
       Eastern Woodlands. *American Antiquity* 41:360–364.

Whittaker, William E., and William Green

2010   Early and Middle Woodland Earthwork Enclosures in Iowa.
       North American Archaeologist 31:27–57.

68 Fort Madison — Under Siege Again

※ Fort Madison, Lee County

※ Historic (1808–1813)

※ SITE NUMBER 13LE10

FORT MADISON IS arguably the most important historical site in Iowa. It was the first U.S. military fort on the Upper Mississippi, the scene of the only real military battle in Iowa, the place where Black Hawk first fought against the United States, and the site of the first U.S. military cemetery. The defeat of forces stationed at the fort in 1813 by Indians delayed American settlement of Iowa by 20 years. In a just world, Fort Madison and its battlefield site would be a well-tended shrine in a park. Instead, it lies beneath crumbling parking lots, with its owners willing to develop and destroy the site.

Fort Madison's history did not begin auspiciously. After the Louisiana Purchase of 1803, the U.S. government wanted to establish control over the enormous territory it had just acquired, so it built three forts: Fort Bellefontaine near St. Louis in 1804, Fort Osage along the Missouri in 1808, and Fort Madison along the Upper Mississippi also in 1808. Fort Madison was poorly situated; instead of occupying a high, defensible bluff, it was built on a river terrace below a bluff. Established Indian tribes of the region did not welcome the American military presence. The Sauk were especially angry with the Americans, having been pressured into ceding their homelands in Illinois in 1804. From the beginning, the fort was under attack. Its poor location meant that it had to be redesigned, and several additional blockhouses built to protect it. The Sauk besieged the fort from a ravine close by to the west, where fighters such as Black Hawk could attack the fort with ease. Attacks became more serious during the War of 1812. Numerous soldiers were killed during the attacks, and most were probably buried close by, since toward the end U.S. forces could not even leave the fort to collect firewood. In late 1813, the fort was abandoned and burned. Iowa was considered Indian country afterward, and not until 1834 would a permanent military presence be reestablished in Iowa and Euroamerican settlement begin.

When settlers arrived at the old fort site in the 1830s, they named their new town Fort Madison in its honor. In 1965, construction work at the parking lot just west of the main Sheaffer Pen Company building encountered what appeared to be parts of the old fort. The University of Iowa began excavating the site that year, and the researchers documented the central blockhouse and much of the interior of the fort. Much of the city volunteered or watched the excavation. Pride in the fort was so high that it was partially reconstructed at the State Fair in Des Moines, and the entire fort was reconstructed on the Fort Madison riverfront to the southwest of the original site.

Alas, the euphoria was soon forgotten, and so was the fort. After the Sheaffer Pen factory closed in 2007, the properties changed hands several times; the factory parcel with the fort remains was split from the battlefield. While Sheaffer Pen had been a good steward of the property, the new

Fort Madison obelisk marker and current above-ground locations of fort, battleground, and burial area, Lee County.

Artist's reconstruction of Fort Madison showing stockade under construction, Lee County. David Session, artist.

owners made plans either to develop the property or to sell to developers. They placed a large sign on the battlefield listing it for sale. After discussions with the new owners proved unsuccessful, preservationists launched a campaign to let the public know about the significance of the fort and battlefield; this campaign made national news. Eventually, the owner of the factory and the fort remains met with archaeologists and seemed sympathetic, but as of this writing still had yet to agree to preserve what is left of the fort. The owners of the battlefield likewise refused to agree to preservation but did allow the OSA to excavate several test trenches in the area in 2009 to determine if there was any chance of preservation. The OSA made 13 trenches in the battlefield, and exposed the original ravine used by Black Hawk and other Indians to attack the fort. Other trenches revealed that parts of the battlefield remained intact.

The battlefield's owners gave the site to the local Catholic school system in 2012, and part of the lot has since been developed into a store, fortunately the main part of the battlefield has not been developed yet. As this book was being finalized, the fort and the battlefield are still up for sale, and may be developed. Attempts to get them listed in the American Battlefield Protection Program, the best hope for preservation, have been blocked because of bureaucratic rules. It is very possible that Iowa will soon lose one of its most important historical sites forever.

✴ TO VISIT

An excellent full-scale reproduction fort and museum is located along the riverfront on Riverview Drive. The fort ruins are under the parking lot just east of the old Sheaffer Pen building, at the corner of 4th Street and old U.S. Highway 61, now Avenue H/State Highway 2; the fort extended south of the highway. A grand obelisk monument is located at the south edge of the fort site, placed unintentionally at the probable location of the southwest blockhouse. The battlefield is located to the east, in the east half of the block bordered by 4th Street, Avenue H, 6th Street, and Avenue G.

✴ WANT TO LEARN MORE?

Doershuk, John F., Joe A. Artz, Cynthia L. Peterson, and
William E. Whittaker
2012   Defining Battlefield Archaeological Context at Fort Madison, Iowa.
       Midcontinental Journal of Archaeology 37:219–242.

McKusick, Marshall B.
2009   Fort Madison, 1808–1813. In *Frontier Forts of Iowa: Indians, Traders,
       and Soldiers, 1682–1862*, ed. William E. Whittaker, 55–74. Iowa City:
       University of Iowa Press.

INDEX